THE ENGLISH BIBLE

1534–1859

THE ENGLISH BIBLE
1534-1859

Peter Levi

'Worship God: for the testimonie of
Jesus, is the spirit of prophecie.'

(Rev 19, 10. Geneva 1560)

WILLIAM B. EERDMANS PUBLISHING COMPANY

Grand Rapids, Michigan

Library of Congress Cataloging in Publication Data

Bible. English. Selections. 1974.
  The English Bible: from Wycliffe to William Barnes.

    1. Bible. English – Versions. I. Levi, Peter, comp. II. Title.
BS391.2.L48 1974 220.5′2 73–23038
ISBN 0–8028–3446–9

For
John and Eirian Wain

CONTENTS

INTRODUCTION

The series of translations of the Bible into English that appeared in the sixteenth and early seventeenth centuries is interesting in several ways. Since the Authorized Version, that is the King James Bible of 1611, was largely a conflation of existing versions, it is of some interest to see what these earlier versions were like, and what kind of orthodoxy of English style or of scriptural interpretation the Authorized Version embodies. It has not been noticed by many scholars that in the series of old Bibles the same very long text demanding a wide range of language was translated in several generations with crucial differences of style; these Bibles are therefore among the best witnesses we have to the development of written English in what was surely its most important formative period. Better still, the witnesses are unconscious; the polemics of one translator against another were not at all concerned with style, but always with accuracy, a preoccupation which is best understood in the light of a prevailing belief in the literal divine inspiration of every word, and even every punctuation, of the scriptures. There was a wish to be clear and to teach, and at least among the bishops to be solemn, but many of the differences of English between the versions represent differences of generation. They also represent important social differences, and the history of the republications and comparative popularity of different Bibles both before and after 1611 throws a significant light on the division of classes that reached its climax in the reign of Cromwell.

These are large claims. But for the proper analysis of what can be contributed by old Bibles to social history and to the history of the language, any small selection will be insufficient, nor can I myself claim to have undertaken the study which this subject merits on a sufficient scale or over a long enough period. I have been interested mostly by the great literary merit of little-known versions, and I have tried in general to present each of them at its best rather than in competition for purposes of comparison; in allowing more space to some versions than to others I wished to offer most of what was least familiar, and of what I thought most excellent. I hope it will not be thought that this is an exercise in propagating 'the Bible as literature'; it is always a mistake to read anything as 'literature', just as it would be to write poems as 'literature'; a writer should mean what he says and a book should be read for what it is. One would object to 'Shakespeare as literature' or still more to 'Homer as literature' quite as much, though about the phrase 'the Bible as literature' there hangs in addition a suspicion of oily and underhand religious or anti-religious polemic. The Bible must inevitably be studied as other religious and prophetic and ancient historical books are studied, but the English Bible is also the almost complete embodiment of the English language, second only perhaps to the works of Shakespeare. In its range and in the use we have made of it, one could say it was an epic; there is no other English national epic.

It was Vico, long before the findings of modern scholarship on the living transmission of epic poetry, who first suggested that in some way Homeric poetry was the creation and self-expression of the whole Greek people over several generations. There is a sense in which the same can be said of the English Bible, not that it was recited or modified as living language in many performances: indeed the imitation of rival or earlier versions in later ones imposed a similarity of language in successive Bibles more than the most punctilious accuracy would account for: but language and its developments and changes over a hundred or more years, and above all the tone and style and vocabulary of language that people approve and will listen to, are inevitably the common creation of everyone who speaks that language. The roots of language and its important modifications are in speech, which after all is a kind of social behaviour, before they are registered in written literature. The English language about 1600 was the uniquely full and true self-expression of the English people of the sixteenth century; a language is never newly created for or in any great work of literature, but we take our words from the teeth and tongues of the dead and the anonymous. But the English Bible is also not unlike an epic poem in that it presents almost the whole range of values and implicit moral feelings that its commonly created language embodies, and, because of its power as language, not only its authority as religious teaching, it can be read with recognition by any native English speaker. We know that this was so, and that the English Bible, though not necessarily always the Authorized Version, has modified and influenced developments in the English language long after 1611. As language, the English Bible has been for many generations until now the mirror of English self-identity. Since religion is so often a principle of national unity, and has been so in fact in England, its expression in a work of such linguistic authority and range has been crucially important. The majesty which has seemed to belong to the Bible has rested on this coincidence of popular creation and moral authority. Once again there is an analogy with Homer. To speak of literary excellence as an explanation of authority of this kind is to introduce a term which itself would need to be broken down and further explained; the virtues of the English Bible are virtues of English language.

Questions about the nature of divine inspiration are outside the scope of this introduction, although I should wish baldly to record that I believe the Bible, and that in judging and discussing versions of it this is bound to have sharpened the edge of my opinions. The most modern English versions are none of them convincing on the level of language; I find this morally and intellectually confusing, since I find it means I am incapable of taking seriously anything that they say. Since I cannot think that I am unique in this experience, I am forced to regard the new versions as ill-judged, and their imposition as an act of folly. I am clear that the principles of English style are a moral matter, not just a question of taste. Reticence, clarity and sobriety, strength and simplicity, logical coherence and a decent habit of speech have their foundations in moral sensibility. The modern English Bibles are written in the language, or the non-language, of a class, and of a class that has no authority in spoken English; but the lives of the early translators, even the bishops, made them, at least in their childhood and youth and perhaps always, more familiar with the living speech of the people than with written books or with middle-class habits of speech, if any such habits existed in the sixteenth century.

Perhaps it is possible to make class distinctions of speech in the prose scenes of Shakespeare, but the distinctions are relatively slight. Today we have been cut off by our society from the roots of a lively and traditional language; what is being created now as English language is still inchoate and obscure, nor do we know whether any work of epic authority as language can ever be created in it again. But a study of early versions of the Bible gives one some reason to hope, since it appears that the proper virtues of the language have not altered so very much even now, but have simply been disregarded, as happened often in the past, and will reassert themselves as they did then. The nineteenth-century revisers of the Authorized Version found frequent passages where Tyndale's version of 1534 seemed preferable in 1880 to what King James' committee had substituted for it in 1611. I could hope for no better fate for this small anthology of versions than that it should suggest something similar if radical work ever begins again on an English Bible.

The reasons why one Bible drove out another in popular use, or why one was commissioned to drive out another, may have varied more than we think. It was not only an Erasmian preoccupation with the claim to accurate scholarship, but there were continuous examples of foreign Biblical translation, and at least in the second half of the sixteenth century the theological tendency of the notes that went with the text of each Bible might contribute as much to make it popular as the clarity of the prose it was written in. Indeed if clarity were the one criterion Tyndale's version of most of what he undertook has hardly been bettered to this day. Then the question of the physical appearance and the type-faces of early Bibles ought not to be neglected. A revised version of the Wycliffite Bible had circulated in numerous manuscript copies in the first twenty years of the sixteenth century. Tyndale's 1525 New Testament was an octavo printed on white vellum with illuminated initials, but the 1534 revision was smaller and fatter, set in a less beautiful type and printed on paper, but still with elaborate initials and miniatures: it was a more workaday book altogether. Coverdale's Bible of 1535, Matthew's Bible of 1537, Henry VIII's Great Bible of 1539

and the Bishops' Bible of 1568 were all tall and fat blackletter folios; so it seems possible that the small but legible
roman type and the easier quarto size of the Geneva Bible
(1560) may have contributed to make it more popular.
These big official and royally licensed Bibles were designed
as solemn books, to be read in churches; their physical
appearance has some of the same properties as their prose.
When Coverdale's Bible was revised in 1537, it was still
the only complete Bible in English except for Matthew's
Bible, which was printed, probably in Antwerp, in the same
year, just as Coverdale's first edition had been in Cologne;
what is significant is that the revised Coverdale was issued
by James Nicholson of Southwark twice in the same year,
first in folio and then in quarto. One may doubt whether
any big blackletter folio book could have circulated widely
in England after the 1530s, particularly if an alternative
was available. Yet as late as 1611 the Authorized Version
appeared in blackletter text, with roman type for the title
page and the introduction; the solemn impression made
may be the reason why in 1613 there were two new printings
of the Geneva Bible, one in its usual type but the other in
blackletter.

The conflict between popular and official Bibles had also
a certain political colour from the beginning. The fear of
heresy and of unofficial, sectarian religion which the Bible
in English might propagate if it got among the common
people was more a matter of politics than of religious
orthodoxy; it was a typical expression of the inner fears
of the governing class at a time when society seemed on
the verge of breaking up. John Wycliffe was already a
famous ideologist before the Wycliffite Bible was produced,
and there is an obvious political resonance in his conception
of a 'dominion of grace', by which every individual is
responsible for his own behaviour to God alone and

immediately. He believed instinctively and strongly in the
righteousness of the poor, and by a confusion of late
medieval theories of property with a somewhat Franciscan
vision of the divine authority of the truly just on earth, he
came to think that the good and just had a natural right to
dominion over the whole sensible world, limited only by the
divine authority of kings. Naturally the political results of
this doctrine and the social conflict which was its context in
the real world went beyond his understanding and his life-
time. He was condemned for heresy at Oxford in 1382, and
he and the travelling preachers who were his disciples were
held responsible for the peasants' revolt of 1381; some of
his followers went so far as to justify the execution of the
Archbishop of Canterbury by Wat Tyler. When Wycliffe
set his friends to translate the Bible into English in the
late fourteenth century, the circulation of the English text
was only one part of the programme of a popular movement
that seemed to take away moral power from the Church
and consequently also from the whole structure of the state,
even though Wycliffe himself took the same view of royal
supremacy as Henry VIII. It is hardly an exaggeration to say
that what was begun by Wycliffe was not finished until the
Levellers were crushed under Cromwell, and perhaps not
even then. The state's immediate answer was the statute
De heretico comburendo, which was passed in 1401.

John Wycliffe died in retirement eighteen months after
his condemnation; his heirs the Lollards were attacked,
persecuted and burnt alive, but they spread as far as Scotland
and had not been stamped out even as late as the reign of
Henry VIII, so that about two hundred manuscripts of
Lollard Bibles have survived to this day; Luther was feared
in England exactly because his doctrines might put new
life into English Lollardry; the circulation of English
versions of the Bible was feared for the same reason, and

was strictly forbidden by law in 1408, which is why Tyndale's New Testament was printed at Cologne and Worms, Coverdale's Bible at Cologne, and Matthew's Bible at Antwerp. But there is no doubt that Lollard Bibles circulated widely, particularly among the country squires and particularly in the later revised version by Wycliffe's secretary John Purvey, who did his work at the beginning of the fifteenth century. It was probably of this Bible that St Thomas More wrote, in his *Dialogue Concerning Heresies*, that 'myself have seen, and can shew you, Bibles fair and old written in English, which have been known and seen by the Bishop of the diocese, and left in laymen's hands, and women's'. If this is true, he must certainly have been ignorant that the translation was Wycliffite, since he was fiercely opposed to everything Wycliffe stood for, and fully approved of the burning of a marked or underlined copy of the Wycliffite Bible in the case of Richard Hun, so it is interesting that he goes on to explain that bishops allowed English Bibles to 'such as he knew for good Catholic folk. But of truth, all such as are found in the hands of heretics, they use to take away'. More's failure to recognize Wycliffite Bibles if the subversive passages were not marked is not unique; one of the surviving Wycliffite manuscripts belonged to Henry vi, another was annotated by the Archbishop of Canterbury. In 1528 when More wrote his *Dialogue* the English Bible was no longer necessarily a symbol or instrument of populism; less than ten years afterwards it could be printed in London with the King's picture and licence; Thomas More in his turn had been beheaded by then for resisting state supremacy in religion. Populism and resistance to the King's authority were both political crimes.

The first Wycliffite Bible was almost as literal as a linear gloss. Possibly this was because the Bible had significance as the supreme source of law for the anti-clerical party which mustered under John of Gaunt, and as a law-book it had to be translated with minute accuracy. The translation was made from Latin, between 1380 and 1384. There exists also one manuscript of an abridged Bible which appears to represent an intermediate stage between this stiff and strange text and John Purvey's revision: it was discovered and studied in the 1950s, and one would wish to know much more about it, but it has not been published. With John Purvey's revision, which perhaps owed as much to Wycliffe's inspiration as the earlier version did, we are in a new world of excellent English. His purpose was to make the Bible 'true and open', and the characteristic properties of his prose are its plainness and clarity as English. One has no idea how courtly Chaucer was until one reads John Purvey's Bible and remembers that they were contemporaries. With some regret I have excluded him from this anthology, not only because a new edition is desirable, which would chart the many variants and modifications that exist in the manuscripts, but because the problems of spelling and pronunciation, and sometimes of the forms of words, make it impossible to modernize this text without travesty, and I was reluctant to print what readers unused to the English of an earlier age might have difficulty in reading. In every later case I have simply modernized spellings and expanded abbreviations, believing that the gain of doing so out-weighs the considerable loss, at least for the purposes of this book: nor can I think that John Purvey would have advised otherwise. His own role was the happiest and best that any writer could hope for: he was dissolved into the people and the language in such a way that he gave power and life to what was most fruitful in the history of both for several hundred years.

The first new version after John Purvey's apart from

some stray pieces of no great distinction embedded in
Caxton's *Golden Legend* was written more than a hundred
years later by William Tyndale. Tyndale's motive is clearly
expressed in a famous story in Foxe's *Book of Martyrs*:
someone said in the 1520s 'We were better be without
God's law than the Pope's', and then Tyndale answered 'I
defy the Pope and all his laws. If God spare my life, ere
many years I will cause a boy that driveth the plough shall
know more of the Scripture than thou dost.' Professor
Bruce has pointed out that Tyndale's splendid and angry
remark reflects some sentences in Erasmus's preface to the
Greek New Testament. When Tyndale came to write his
new translation he used, with some reference to the Latin
Vulgate and to Luther's German version, the third, 1522,
edition of Erasmus's Greek. Luther's German New Testament also appeared in 1522; in that year Tyndale left
Cambridge for a country tutorship in Gloucestershire, and
made the first English translation of Erasmus's *Enchiridion,*
one of the seminal works of reformed religion. In 1523 he
applied to the Bishop of London for patronage while he
translated the New Testament; his hope was disappointed,
and in 1524 he left England for Germany. The work was
finished in about a year, and eighty pages of it had already
been printed in Cologne when the city senate heard of its
existence and forbade the printer to carry on. The book was
finally printed complete at Worms in February 1526. One
copy of the first sixty-four pages of the unfinished book
from Cologne has also survived; the prologue, which was
not reprinted at Worms, contained long unacknowledged
quotations in English from the German prologue to
Luther's New Testament. As many copies as the Bishop of
London could collect of the Worms edition were cere-
monially burnt at St Paul's Cross in October of 1526, and
so scholarly a reformist as Thomas More wrote against

Tyndale in 1529 and again in 1532. Tyndale himself was kidnapped in Antwerp in 1535 by agents of the Emperor Charles v, and in spite of protests from the court of England he was strangled and his body burnt in 1536; when he died Coverdale's complete Bible, which owed him a debt and was Lutheran in about the same sense and to the same degree as his own work, was already circulating freely in England with the King's spoken permission and the patronage of Anne Boleyn and Thomas Cromwell.

Tyndale's missionary zeal to translate the Bible into English certainly owed much more to Erasmus than to Wycliffe; essentially what Tyndale undertook was to carry out part of the programme of changes that Erasmus demanded. The opposition of Thomas More and of the Bishop of London had something to do with their fear of disruptive foreign heresies and of English Lollardry, but inevitably Tyndale triumphed. His victory was one of plain English prose style; strength and simplicity often go together, but seldom with the extraordinary life that Tyndale commanded, particularly in his revised New Testament of 1534. This must to some degree embody the handsomeness of the plain English of his time, and of an inevitably country habit of speech in the mouth of a learned and passionate man. The passion to be understood was radical in him, and it has given a sense of necessity to his language, as if it could hardly have been written otherwise. But its freshness and exactness were not inevitable, they were chosen and achieved; in John Fisher's version some of the psalms which were printed in 1545 belong to the same years as Tyndale's New Testament, yet there is a striking difference of tone. The differences between the original 1525 text and the 1534 revision are not enormously far-reaching, but they do show great improvements, and they make it possible to see how his mind was working.

'Blessed are the maintainers of the peace' in 1525 became 'Blessed are the peacemakers' in 1534; 'See that your light so shine' became 'Let your light so shine'; 'The favour of our Lord' became 'The grace of our Lord'; 'And ye shall find ease unto your souls' became 'And ye shall find rest unto your souls'. In the description of the Last Supper in 1525 'Jesus took bread, gave thanks, brake it and gave it to them and said' but in 1534 'Jesus took bread, blessed and brake and gave to them and said'. The earlier version is close to Luther's. In the praises of love in the twelfth chapter of the first epistle to the Corinthians there was nearly no significant change, because there the 1525 version was already perfect; the Authorized Version follows it closely, with some changes which are not improvements: in 1611 charity was substituted for love. The passages printed in this anthology are taken from the Cambridge 1938 reprint of Tyndale's 1534 revision: the Cambridge edition also reprints the 1525 version wherever it differs from 1534.

Between 1525 and 1530 Tyndale translated from a Hebrew text the first five books of the Old Testament, and in 1531 the Book of Jonah; these works he published at once, and in his 1534 New Testament he included translations of the epistles of the year taken from the Old Testament. After his death some translations of his from historical books of the Old Testament (Joshua to 2 Chronicles) were included in Matthew's Bible in 1537, so that it looks as if Tyndale had intended to translate the entire Bible and left some material towards it which was known to other Protestant scholars. In his Old Testament translations he wrote with a fluent boldness and strength, though not perhaps with the solemn and delicate simplicity of his gospels. The Bible after all is not one but many books, and it demands a very wide range of style. It is one of the greatest tragedies in the history of our language that Tyndale was not let live to complete his Bible translation. If his English is compared in range and strength with that of Sir Thomas More, it will survive that hard test triumphantly. What Erasmus expressed as a rhapsodical hope in the Latin preface to a Greek text, Tyndale's language went a long way to accomplish in England, that the New Testament should begin to become a familiar book to women as well as men, and to the poor as well as the educated. His 1534 version is the true criterion of the kind of English in which we still feel the New Testament should be written, and it is often a touchstone for the achievement of later English Bibles.

Tyndale was born five or six years before the end of the fifteenth century and was hardly more than forty when he died; Myles Coverdale was seven years older and lived to be eighty-one; most of his work was done after Tyndale's, some of it long after, but his English is that of the same generation and has the same delicate and deliberate strength, the same linen texture. Like Luther, he was once an Augustinian, but he left his order; from 1528 until 1535 and again from 1540 to 1547 he lived in exile from England, his five English years being those of the ascendancy of Thomas Cromwell. He came back for the reign of Edward vi and for two years he was Bishop of Exeter, but in 1553 he was lucky to escape burning and lived again in exile until 1559. By this time he was an old man, and in any case too extreme a Puritan to expect promotion under the early Elizabethan settlement; he took part in Parker's consecration as Archbishop of Canterbury, wearing a plain black gown without vestments, he was not reappointed to Exeter, and in 1566 he resigned the living of St Magnus in London on a question of liturgical conformity, though he continued to preach half privately with famous success until his death.

Coverdale started with no ambition to translate the Bible, but he had worked for a time under Tyndale at

Hamburg, and then in 1534, a year before the shadows closed in around Tyndale, Cromwell's ascendancy was sealed by More's execution, and it became vital to produce a Protestant Bible quickly in English. Coverdale was 'boldened in God to labour faithfully in the same'. At exactly this time pirated and debased editions of Tyndale's New Testament were beginning to circulate; the 1534 revision was intended to obliterate them, and it seems to have been successful. Coverdale worked swiftly, translating 'out of Douche and Latyn', and his complete Bible was printed at Cologne in 1535, and paid for by an Antwerp merchant who must certainly have been Tyndale's friend. Coverdale seems to have used the Latin Vulgate and a Dominican Latin version of 1528, and also Luther's Bible, but his work depended most heavily on the Zürich Bible of 1531, which was a Swiss German adaptation of Luther, and in the New Testament on Tyndale. Copies that reached England had a dedication to Henry VIII added, which was printed in Southwark, and the King permitted them to circulate. It was a patchwork, and in point of scholarship it could hardly expect to hold the field for ever, but in the language and in English social history it was an important document. Nor was it by any means Coverdale's only or his most lasting contribution to English Bible translation. The official Great Bible of 1539 was his work, so was its revised second edition in 1540; the Psalms as they were reprinted in the Book of Common Prayer and as they are still in use in the services of the Church of England are Coverdale's Psalms. The Psalms of the Authorized Version are less satisfying and we are fortunate that they have never driven Coverdale's out of public use or national tradition. Even this was not the end of his labours, since Coverdale was in Geneva in 1558, and contributed something at least to the Geneva Bible of 1560. It will be best to treat his work on the later Bibles in the order in which each Bible appeared in print, but even had he died in 1535 when he was fifty the importance of his achievement would still be great; he was a better writer and preacher in his native language than scholar in ancient ones, it is possible that in his old age his corrections were towards a solemnity and smoothness which is less morally attractive than the sap and sunlight of Tyndale, but his language was strong and venerable, and any preference that may be felt for later versions will be for the English of a different generation, perhaps for a later development of the language to which in his prose style Coverdale was already pointing.

None of the early Bible translators ended their lives peacefully; Coverdale at least contrived to die in bed, but the real compiler of Matthew's Bible was John Rogers, who was burnt to death under Queen Mary in 1555. Rogers had known Tyndale well, and very possibly worked with him at the Old Testament historical books. His new Bible was put together from Tyndale's unpublished work supplemented from Coverdale, and paid for by London merchants and printers. Cranmer obtained a royal licence for it through Thomas Cromwell in 1537, and a similar licence was issued for the second edition of Coverdale, which also appeared in London in the same year. Thomas Matthew was a pen-name, hardly more than a fiction, since at least one book of the Old Testament in Matthew's Bible, the prophecy of Malachi, was actually signed W. T. There was naturally a royal dedication, and Rogers equipped his book with notes and references and even some renderings of the text from the French Bibles of Lefèvre (1534) and Olivetan (1535). But effectively what he was producing was as nearly as possible a posthumous Bible in English by Tyndale, who was one year dead. Now the tide had turned; Cranmer and the King were both anxious for a national English Bible; Thomas Cromwell was still in power, though Anne Boleyn, who seems to have favoured Coverdale, was beheaded in 1536; Matthew's Bible was being received in parish churches with an enthusiasm that was already out of hand, so that the King and the Archbishop moved to suppress a new custom of reading it aloud while service was going on at the altar; at the same time some of the clergy and the bishops were frightened by its Protestant notes. This is how it came about that Myles Coverdale was commissioned to make a more official revision not of his own but of Matthew's, that is Tyndale's Bible, which was to be printed in Paris and copies kept in all English churches. Printing started in the summer of 1538; it was delayed by the confiscation of the sheets by the French authorities, but type and paper and printers were brought to England, and in 1539 the Great Bible of Henry VIII appeared, with its preface by Archbishop Cranmer.

Coverdale's work of revision is of some interest. Sometimes he loses his own clarity of 1535 in an attempt to compromise with Tyndale. It may be thought this was in the interest of scholarship, and it should be remembered that the Great Bible was censored and supervised by English bishops, including the same Cuthbert Tonstall who had burnt Tyndale's New Testament at St Paul's Cross only thirteen years before. Coverdale's own Bible had been newly revised by Richard Taverner. The intellectual atmosphere of the England of these years was both repressive and confused; it is vividly conveyed in Wyatt's first satire and by the lament for the suitors of Anne Boleyn written after their execution: 'The axe is down, their heads are in the street.' To speak more technically and perhaps more substantially, Coverdale was employed to revise what was already a patchwork quilt of revisions, and to embody in his revision the conflicting motives of a blunt but confused monarch, a Lutheran chancellor and a devious episcopacy. So where Coverdale had written in 1535 'His eyes were not dim, and his cheeks were not fallen'. he must now base himself on Tyndale's rendering 'His eyes were not dim nor his cheeks abated', so he produced 'His eyes were not dim, nor his natural colour abated'. Coverdale sometimes corrected Tyndale to a more solemn prose. 'And the Lord was with Joseph, and he was a lucky fellow' became 'And God was with Joseph and he became a lucky man'. Often he profited from Tyndale, but seldom improved on him, except maybe towards a prosaic plainness and a kind of dead clarity. This is a harsh judgement, and one makes it with pain; it is true that in the minute subtleties of rhythm Coverdale was perhaps supreme, and that one hears English better with his ears; but we must bitterly regret what was lost, and no doubt the people did regret it. The price of the Great Bible was not small; it was fixed by proclamation in May 1541 at ten shillings unbound or twelve shillings trimmed, bound and clasped. In 1543 Tyndale's translation was forbidden by law, and the common people were forbidden absolutely to read the Bible. Coverdale and Tyndale Bibles were publicly burnt in London, and Convocation at Canterbury demanded a revision of the Great Bible to make it agree with the Latin Vulgate. Fortunately this revision was never finished. There is a note in a copy of an English edition of Polydore Vergil, written in Gloucestershire a few months before the King's death:

'At Oxford the year 1546 brought down to Seynbury by John Darby price 14d when I kept Mr. Latymers sheep I bought this book when the testament was abrogated that shepherds might not read it I pray God amend that blindness. Writ by Robert Williams keeping sheep upon Seynbury hill 1546.'

Under Edward VI the Great Bible was once again commanded to be installed in churches, with an English version of a paraphrase by Erasmus kept beside it, and in 1549 and 1553 it was reprinted; but Coverdale's translation was also reprinted, once in 1550 and once in 1553, and in 1551 Bishop Becke dedicated to King Edward a new edition of Taverner's revision of Coverdale's Old with Tyndale's New Testament. The same years saw the book of Common Prayer in English and the foundation of new schools for godliness and good learning. They were better years for people like Robert Williams, but no original work was done in them in the translation of scripture except for an excessively eccentric and donnish manuscript version of St Matthew by the King's tutor, Sir John Cheke, which remained very properly unprinted until 1843. Edward reigned for six years, Queen Mary for five. She burnt Cranmer and John Rogers alive, and Coverdale survived in exile only through the intervention of the King of Denmark and the diplomacy of his own curiously named relative, Maccabaeus Macalpine. The official Great Bible lived on through these storms into the early years of Elizabeth; it had never been condemned or gone back on, and it was still for sale when Mary died in 1558: it had to be reprinted again only in 1562. But when Mary drove the Protestants abroad in 1553 she became the unconscious and unwilling patron of the most powerful of all English Bibles, the Geneva version of 1560. It was the work of the exiles in Geneva, particularly William Whittingham and Anthony Gilby; when Elizabeth came to the throne it was almost ready to be printed, and the psalms were published at once in honour of the coronation. Whittingham's New Testament had already appeared in 1557, and an earlier attempt at the psalms in the same year.

The Geneva version is undoubtedly a capable translation

written by scholars: it was made with close attention to Hebrew originals, and with some use of the Hebrew commentary of David Kimchi, among many other sources. Geneva in the fifties saw new editions of the Latin Vulgate, of the Greek and Hebrew texts, the Bible in Italian and in Spanish, and more than twenty of the Bible in French; already in the forties it had seen a Jewish version from Hebrew into Latin. In comparison with all this the English enterprise must have appeared small, but it was strongly based in original scholarship; indeed it can hardly be separated from the intellectual culture of Geneva at the time, 'in respect of this ripe age and clear light which God hath now revealed'. Their English was not so measured as to be melodious, but it had a powerful music that must always belong to the language when it is spoken with lucid intellectual passion: and in 1560 at possibly the most promising moment in its history, twenty or thirty years before its fullest ripeness. Argument, prophecy and narrative run in powerful syntactic streams, and this version more than any other makes a continuous and passionate sense of the Bible. The English is popular, straight, never hieratic or grandiose, still in the tradition of Tyndale and full of the 'lively phrase of the Hebrew'.

It has often been suggested that the important difference between versions of the Bible was in the theological tendency of the notes that went with the text. It seems doubtful whether that alone could account for the immediate and overwhelming popularity of the Geneva Bible. Between 1560 and the appearance of the Authorized Version in 1611 Tyndale's New Testament was reprinted five times, the Great Bible seven, the Bishops' Bible that succeeded it twenty-two, and the Geneva Bible over a hundred and twenty, an average of two or three new editions a year. Even the Authorized Version failed to drive it out; in 1616

27

Laud forbade it to be printed any more in England, so that from that year on it was printed in Amsterdam. Over sixty new editions of the Geneva Bible or the Geneva New Testament appeared after 1611. It was the Bible of Shakespeare from about 1596 and the Bible of Milton, it survived well into the mid-century as the popular Bible of Scotland and took root in America with the Pilgrim Fathers in 1620. It was the source of the Soldier's Pocket Bible, which was sixteen pages of fighting texts that Oliver Cromwell printed for the army in 1643. It was naturally Bunyan's Bible. The reason why it ceased to be printed after about 1644 and almost ceased to be remembered after about 1700 is political and social: it was identified with forces in English society which were stifled in those years. A last stray edition exists to prove it was not quite forgotten in 1778. The theological notes must have had some importance, particularly at first, and their influence can apparently be traced both on Shakespeare and on Milton, but the powerful vitality of this Bible had a deeper and more spiritual source than footnotes, since I suppose it may be said that language is nobler and more spiritual in its nature than theological tendency, and more substantial in its reality. As to its excellence, the old judgement of the common people should still be taken seriously by us.

It was a handsome quarto printed in Geneva in roman type, which had never before been used for the Bible in English; the English church at Geneva paid for it, and in 1561 John Bodley, the father of the founder of the library at Oxford, was licensed by the Queen to print it for seven years. He produced at once a big folio edition. In the early Geneva Bibles the theological notes seem to us today to be clearly phrased but really unaggressive; an extremer Protestantism with some translated anti-papal tirades was introduced in the editions of the nineties, under the influence of Walsingham, whose secretary Lawrence Tomson had revised the New Testament in 1576 and added notes by Beza and Camerarius. Still, the 1560 notes were already uncompromising. There is a note about a king who deposed his mother for idolatry, 'Herein he shewed that he lacked zeal, for she ought to have died', and another on 'the rod of my son' in Ezekiel, 'Meaning, the sceptre: shewing, that it will not spare the King who should be as the son of God, and in his place'. The note on 'I will spare them' in Malachi is 'That is, forgive their sins, and govern them with my Spirit'. There is surely as much of rebellious popular feeling as there is of Calvinism about these notes; one should remember that Geneva itself was intended for a republic of the just. It is no surprise that the notes annoyed James 1. There are some splendidly sharp sayings about the Papacy even in the first edition in the notes to Revelation. 'He describeth Rome to be the sink of all abomination and devilishness, and a kind of hell.' When horses and chariots are mentioned there is a sudden glimpse of a baroque street scene as it appeared to Genevan eyes, and no doubt to generations of English peasants: 'Such as the wantons use at Rome'. The later notes are more elaborate and flatter, But Tomson's revision had an influence, since it was often reprinted as the Geneva New Testament. There may have been some official feeling against the Geneva notes in England from the beginning since Archbishop Parker in a memorandum to the Bishops' Bible translators warned them 'to make no bitter notes on any text', but that was at an early period of the Elizabethan settlement, before Catholic fellow-travellers had become negligible in the English Church.

With the wide circulation and great popularity of the Geneva Bible one might have felt that a peak had been reached, but the Archbishop still wanted an official substitute. He made no move to ban the Geneva version or to suppress its printing, which he in fact encouraged, and seems not to have wanted to drive it out, which anyway would surely have been impossible. He proposed that some bishops of his province and one or two future bishops should revise the Great Bible; this scheme was floated in 1561 and the result published in 1568, once again in black-letter and in folio. The revision was supposed to be entirely a matter of scholarship, to render the discredited passages more accurately by using Latin cribs to the Hebrew text, because the bishops were not able to cope with Hebrew. The nullity and pretension of this enterprise need no further analysis. In 1571 Convocation decreed that bishops and cathedrals and as far as possible churches must possess and use the resulting book, and we can tell from the experience of Shakespeare that they did so, but the Queen had the good sense to show it no further favour, except that of silence. A copy of the Geneva Bible was presented to her in 1583 and we must assume it was acceptable. The Bishops' Bible was twice revised and in some of its later editions Coverdale's psalms, which had held the field in Common Prayer, drove out the bishops' version of 1568 even from their own Bible. The principal objection to the Bishops' Bible is that it superimposed a patchwork on a patchwork yet again, and that the bishops were solemn and incompetent provincial clerics as a pessimist might expect.

The next spark of a natural talent for English in the history of the Bible came from an unexpected source. Now the Catholics were in exile in their turn, and at the end of the century they produced their own Bible. There was little part for it to play in national life. It was printed complete only twice (until very much later), circulated secretly, and was finally massacred in revision by Challenor in the 1740s and by his successors, so that only a very few scholars have ever seen or heard it. Its first English edition was not until 1789, when it was printed in Liverpool. Since I was brought up in English Catholic institutions I knew of its existence and had heard of its virtues, but I seldom had access to it; where the early editions exist they are treasured as monuments of recusancy, and today no ordinary library can afford to buy one. Since Cardinal Wiseman recognized that its revision had been a disimprovement, it is not unreasonable to complain that it is scandalous that it should never have been reprinted in modern times. It has an astonishing life as English, its prose is somewhat Latinate and based on Latin, but wonderfully musical, fresh and sweet-smelling. It is natural in its idioms and completely convincing in its rhythms. Its language is within ten years the English of the generation of Shakespeare, and this of course is its strength. It was written, I myself believe, completely by Gregory Martin except maybe for Maccabees, and overseen by two or three of his colleagues; Gregory Martin was at St John's College, Oxford, for thirteen years with Edmund Campion, one of the best English prose writers of the late sixteenth century; Shakespeare's schoolmaster was an undergraduate in the college during that time, Martin was famous at St John's as 'our Hebraist, our Grecian, our poet'; one ought not to be surprised in view of his background that in exile as a Bible translator he showed something like genius, although often with a scrupulous stiffness which reflects his conservative motive just as the freedom and passion of the Geneva translators reflected their revolutionary motive.

To read most of the discussions of Martin's work, one would think his language terribly constrained by faithfulness to the Latin, but it was very often not so, and even in the psalms, where he translated from the particularly knotty Latin text in church use, his version is sometimes preferable as English to any other; he holds his own with Coverdale. Ronald Knox suggested that Martin's English was simply an alternative language which might in different political circumstances have become as influential and venerable as the Authorized Version. It is true that the judgement by which we prefer the King James Bible is rooted in a sense of language in which that Bible is a fundamental and pervasive influence, but the victorious immediacy of the Geneva Bible, which was little known from 1660 to 1960, suggests another criterion; languages are made by peoples not by Bibles. It is also true that the glossary of new and difficult words at the back of the Douai Bible includes some which have passed into common usage, and the Bible itself includes some phrases which have done the same, but that is unlikely to be due to the influence of the reading of a Catholic Bible in England; it is simply an index of the way in which the language was moving. In the age of Shakespeare English was no longer the plain tongue of the exiles in Geneva; it was language of astonishing abundance and variety, with a thousand growing points like the first shooting of bushes in spring. It would need to be cropped back for a hundred years, and no doubt something would then be lost. Most of the supposed eccentricities of the Douai Bible, and the continental flavour it has been credited with for better or worse, should be understood as a part of that English abundance of language which flowered so profusely in Shakespeare. At that moment there was no grain that the mills of the English language seemed unable to grind. I can only indicate, for I am unable to demonstrate, what I think was the role of the Douai Bible and the way its excellence can best be understood, since the argument depends on an interpretation of the history of the language between the Geneva Bible and Clarendon's *History of the Great Rebellion*. It is typical of the low level to which *odium theologicum* reduced such debates in the past that of six words singled out by King James's committee as examples of deliberate obscurantism, five were the words 'tunic, rational, holocaust, praepuce and pasch'; the sixth is 'Azimes' which is after all a technicality, as is the sense of 'rational' referred to.

Gregory Martin began his work from 1578 at Rheims; money was collected in England by Robert Persons in 1580–1 to the tune of a thousand crowns; the Catholic New Testament was published in 1582 and Persons records that the number of English Catholics doubled in a year. The Old Testament appeared in two compact quarto volumes at Douai in 1609–10. The New Testament was reprinted in 1621 and 1633 and the complete Douai–Rheims Bible only once in 1635. Gregory Martin moved steadily through the Bible at two chapters a day: the Old Testament may have been unfinished when he died in 1584. The chapters were revised as he finished them by William Allen, formerly fellow of Oriel, Cardinal and founder of the Douai college, by Richard Bristow formerly fellow of Exeter, and William Reynolds, formerly fellow of New College. It is a disconcerting truth that the Douai–Rheims Bible might have been written in Oxford. The Rheims New Testament, which was naturally greeted with invective from the establishment's pamphleteers, was taken seriously by the committee for the Authorized Version, who incorporated a surprising number of its readings. The theological notes of Douai and Rheims differ from those of the 1560 Geneva Bible as one might expect, but they are even less aggressive, somewhat devotional and scholastic, and by no means compelling to the attention. They seem to reflect the atmosphere of the Catholic mission in England. 'Men of light conversation, and contemners of Christ shall also be converted, become grave, and greatly honour him.' The house of Rechabites has a note on 'Religious Orders in the Old Testament'. 'An Ecclesiastical preacher must not flatter the people. He must move tears, not laughter.' 'After the reduction of heathenish or heretical people to catholic religion, there will be great want of spiritual pastors.' Such a note has a strange resonance when one comes across it in a thumbed and crumbling volume of 1609.

Finally something must be said about King James's Bible, recently well studied by Professor A. C. Partridge in *English Biblical Translation*. It was yet another attempt to drive out the popular Bible, that is the Geneva Bible, largely for theological but also for social reasons. In this it failed, but later political history succeeded. We are to think not of the exhausted streams of theological ideas, but of the last phases of late medieval populism and the beginnings of English nonconformity, and of where they meet in the mid-seventeenth century. The Authorized Version was a conflation of existing translations; it was supposed to be a revision of the Bishops' Bible, and the manuscript annotations in a 1603 copy of that Bible now in the Bodleian library suggest that essentially it was so, though these annotations have been little studied. The Authorized Version was compelling in its royal authority, in its solemn learning, and in its majestic prose. It stands halfway between the English of the generation of Geneva and that of the generation of Lord Clarendon and the *Eikon Basilike*. It had a certain archaic quality even when it was written, which no doubt arose from the reuse of earlier renderings and was cemented with a deliberate gravity of tone. The Authorized Version has been so much loved in the Church of England from the time of the Restoration, when it was already venerable, and indeed by most of the English nation rich and poor, until the last few years when Church and Bible together have seemed to founder in revisions and reformism, that an outsider can make little headway if he should criticize it. If ever successful establishment prose existed, this is it. Its texture is perfectly smooth and its voice mellow. English writing had moved a long way from Lear in this Bible, and a long way from any but the most courtly speeches of Shakespeare, or from Campion's Brag, or from Tyndale.

When all this is admitted, it was still a most remarkable achievement. The rules for translating were conservative. The Bishops' Bible was to be the basis, old ecclesiastical words like church and baptism were to be kept, and the rule for the forms of names was common use. The only notes were to be scholarly. There were three committees for the Old Testament, two for the New, and one for Apocrypha; two met at Oxford, two at Cambridge and two at Westminster. A committee of twelve, two from each of the first committees, then revised the whole work in nine months, and the final editing was done by Bishop Bilson of Winchester and Miles Smith, later the Bishop of Gloucester, at Stationers' Hall. It goes without saying that neither Donne nor Shakespeare was consulted, but nor was so powerful a scholar and so brilliant a writer in English as Hugh Broughton, who was out of favour with the learned establishment and was not best pleased to be excluded.

A copy of some notes made by John Bois at meetings of the committee of twelve has recently been discovered and published; it confirms the very high opinion one might already have formed about the scholarly capabilities of the committee, particularly of Andrew Downes, the Professor of Greek at Cambridge. The notes show evidence of a familiarity with patristic writings, a consciousness of the work of Scaliger and Casaubon, an ability to quote from memory (not quite accurately) on points of language from Virgil, Horace and Plautus, and above all an intensity of verbal sense both in ancient languages and in English. If one wished to see in what way the constant study of dead languages could enliven a scholar's grasp of English at that time, one could have no clearer proof than these notes. Sometimes they are more impressive than the final version, since not every nuance of an ambiguous word can be carried on a single English equivalent. In the eighteenth chapter of Revelation there are some attractive suggestions which were clearly rejected because the bishops preferred a pure run and a smooth consistency. Downes for example remarked that what the people threw on their heads in verse nineteen was not dust but earth, and that Babylon ought to be thrown down in verse twenty-one 'at one push'. In the opening of chapter seventeen Bois or his colleagues wanted 'I will shew thee that great, damnable harlot', which is surely better than 'the judgement of the great whore'. All these notes, except for Greek words and English renderings, were kept in Latin: can it be that some of the discussions that led to the Authorized Version were carried on in Latin? At any rate, the hypnotic rhythms of King James' Bible are at least as powerful a reflection of classical, particularly Latin learning as the more Latinate vocabulary of Douai.

When the Authorized Version appeared, Hugh Broughton was furious. 'The late Bible . . . was sent to me to censure: which bred in me a sadness that will grieve me while I breathe, it is so ill done. . . . The new edition crosseth me. I require it to be burnt.' He was sixty-two years old, and a Hebrew scholar of attainments so great as to tempt him into eccentricity; it is a pleasing fact that his family bore owls on their coat of arms. He got into controversy and disgrace with the establishment with his *Concent of Scripture* in 1588, an attempt to reconcile the chronology of scripture with what was known from secular historians. He believed that not only every word but every piece of Hebrew punctuation in the Bible was divinely inspired. The bishops forced him overseas, and as early as 1593 he wrote to Lord Burghley to suggest a complete new Bible translation. He did write his own versions of several books of the Bible, but late in his life, and they remained mostly unpublished until 1662. They have the verbal texture of thunder and lightning, and an intellectual texture of sombre and oppressive scholarship constantly enlivened by flashes of intelligence and language. He was genuinely a great and neglected genius; in an earlier age he might have worked on the Geneva Bible, in a later he might have drunk himself to death. He did die soon after 1611; he was 'seized on by the Cough of the Lungs' at Gravesend when he arrived there in November of that year. I have found it true that 'the Author's Writings do carry with them, I know not what, a kind of holy, and happy Fascination, that the serious Reader of them is won upon, by a sweet violence'. His versions of the prophets, in which the Rev. Alexander Gordon, writing in 1886 in the *Dictionary of National Biography*, already discovered 'a majesty of expression', have a strength which in the Authorized Version is drowned in harmonious honey.

There is no need to take equally seriously any of the later translations of the Bible. At the best, they were attempts to clarify speech, and to adapt scripture to the sensibilities of an increasing enlightenment. Had the life of the Church in England been a genuine, organic life, that would have been an important enterprise, but as things were it had no popular roots, since the English language and people remained unenlightened until scholarship had been cut off from common English by class divisions; nor in the England of the eighteenth century could there possibly be official patronage for an enlightened Bible. It is of some interest that Harwood's Liberal Translation and John Wesley's New Testament, a pious and conservative modernization, seem to have appeared in the same year, 1768, although I have traced only the second, 1790, edition of Wesley. Several scholars were working on English New Testaments towards the end of the eighteenth century: Newcome, the Archbishop of Armagh, Kenrick at Exeter and Gilbert Wakefield, another stormy petrel and by far the most interesting of this list. Harwood was the most peculiar: his New Testament was to be 'a *liberal* and *diffusive* version of the sacred classics', to 'induce persons of a liberal education and polite taste to peruse the sacred volume' by employing 'the innocent stratagem of a *modern style*'. The passages I have reproduced are sufficient to show the contradictions implicit in any such enterprise; his successes make one weep for what the English people have suffered even more than his many failures. Wakefield was plain and sober; he differed rather little from the Authorized Version. It seemed to him 'a most ignoble ambition to court the sickly tastes of those readers to whom the native plainness of the gospels has no relish'. Within the limits of a soberly conservative literary sense, Wakefield is a strong and effective writer, though he is perhaps not sufficiently arresting to be quoted here. He was a second wrangler at Cambridge, who thought algebra 'odious beyond comparison', and an ordained deacon, who thought his ordination 'the most disingenuous action of my whole life, utterly incapable of palliation or apology'. He became a dissenter, sympathized strongly with the French Revolution, and led an angry life as a scholar. Porson remarked of him that 'he was as violent against Greek accents as he was against the Trinity'. It is not surprising that his work on the New Testament is more convincing than the dull 1808 revision, which was produced by a scholarly committee.

The atmosphere of that intensely respectable piece of work, the Bodleian copy of which belonged to Lord Norris and remains largely uncut to this day, is fairly conveyed by the note on 'crown of thorns': 'More probably of acanthus, or bearsfoot. The design was to insult, not to torture. See Bp. Pearce.' It does contain an excellent critical introduction on editions of the New Testament in Greek, but its basic text was Archbishop Newcome's, which differed from the Authorized Version mostly to suggest departures from the usual text of the Greek; the committee often returned to the Authorized Version, sometimes to restore euphonious archaisms. This in fact was a less capable predecessor of the Victorian Revised Version, and the principles of its style reached their perfect statement in the introduction to Dean Afford's New Testament: 'a translator of the Holy Scripture must be absolutely colourless'. Solemnity had shifted for a moment with Wakefield and the lamentable Edward Harwood, a possibility had half-opened in the language, but if a chance of a new English Bible really existed at that time, then it was missed.

Benjamin Franklin's few verses from Job were intended as a joke, an anti-monarchic satire, but Matthew Arnold took them seriously and was 'delighted that something at least lay beyond the range of his victorious common sense'. On the other hand his Our Father was intended seriously, and it seems almost as funny today. But the palm of the inappropriate ought to go not to Harwood but to Francis Quarles, for his Sions Sonets (1630), a translation of the Song of Songs, Sions Elegies, which is a version of the Lamentations, and Job Militant, which may just possibly by counter-suggestion have given Milton the title of Samson Agonistes. The Dorset version of the Song of Songs by William Barnes, who was often but not always a better poet than Quarles, was one of a large number of dialect versions of this work based on the Authorized Version commissioned together and printed in the same year, 1859. In the mid-nineteenth century the dense specificity of early and of dialect English was relished because it was being lost. We are a hundred years later, and now our only hope is in a fresh study of the history of our language, to recognize it in its whole substance and its whole history, and to grow new shoots from what we see as genuine and alive.

There are naturally a number of features both of the early and late history of Bible translation in England on which fundamental study still remains to be done, and which I have neglected; it may be exactly these obscurer and more neglected areas where the most enlivening revelations of the history of the language will come to light. I have been told that Thomas More, of whom I have spoken rather harshly because of his attitude to Tyndale, did himself frequently translate scattered passages from scripture when he quoted them in his own works; but the prose works of More have not been completely reprinted since the rare edition of 1554, and I have not worked through them. He was probably the first English advocate of a committee Bible, another black mark perhaps, but the lively intensity of a phrase like 'the infant hopped in her belly' at least bears comparison with Tyndale's 'the babe sprung in her belly', though it may be thought that Tyndale is preferable, since here as elsewhere he achieves liveliness without colloquial eccentricity. There are many sixteenth-century preachers who translate for themselves; Latimer in particular in his sermons gives a clear sense of the way in which the rhythms of a lively translation could relate to the other levels of language surrounding them, and the same skill in the multiple relationships of language is of course to be found in Donne. It is in this aspect more than in any other that the old art, if I may call it an art, of the pulpit comes close to poetry.

The language of the Bible is already a multiple English, the fragments of Bible translation embedded in sermons take on a denser colour and a stranger resonance, but the language is one language, and this is what we must recover. The individual treasures and the writers of genius that such an enterprise will bring to light are enough of a reward to make the research worth while, but the final object of study is the heart and substance of the English language.

I

TYNDALE (1534)

William Tyndale's New Testament exists in a version of
1525, an extremely rare book, and also in a revised and
genuinely improved version of 1534. The text here is taken
from the 1938 edition of the 1534 text, with notes of certain
variants from the older version; these variants have no
authority of course for the 1534 text, but they are presented
simply for purposes of comparison. Tyndale translated
the New Testament from the Greek, but he also included
in his book an appendix of feast-day epistles from the Sarum
rite which come from the Old Testament, and it is useful to
reproduce some at least of his undoubtedly genuine work
as an Old Testament translator. He was barbarously put to
death before he had completed the whole Bible. His 1525
New Testament was reprinted in 1836 and again in 1862,
but the 1534 New Testament not until 1938.

Matthew v. 19–26

Whosoever breaketh one of these least commandments, and
teacheth men so, he shall be called the least in the kingdom
of heaven. But whosoever observeth and teacheth, the same
shall be called great in the kingdom of heaven.[1]

[1] 1525 version: . . . and shall teach men so. . . . But whosoever shall
observe and teach them, that person . . .

For I say unto you, except your righteousness exceed the righteousness of the Scribes and Pharisees, you cannot enter into the kingdom of heaven.

Ye have heard how it was said unto them of the old time: Thou shalt not kill. For whosoever killeth, shall be in danger of judgement. But I say unto you, whosoever is angry with his brother, shall be in danger of judgement. Whosoever sayeth unto his brother Racha, shall be in danger of a counsel. But whosoever sayeth thou fool shall be in danger of hell fire.

Therefore when thou offerest thy gift at the altar, and there rememberest that thy brother hath ought against thee: leave there thine offering before the altar, and go thy way first and be reconciled to thy brother,[1] and then come and offer thy gift.

Agree with thine adversary quickly, whiles thou art in the way with him, lest that adversary deliver thee to the judge, and the judge deliver thee to the minister, and then thou be cast into prison. I say unto thee verily: thou shalt not come out thence till thou have paid the utmost farthing.

Matthew VI. 19–34

See that ye gather you not treasure upon the earth, where rust and moths corrupt, and where thieves break through and steal. But gather ye treasure together in heaven, where neither rust nor moths corrupt, and where thieves neither break up nor yet steal. For wheresoever your treasure is, there will your hearts be also.

The light of the body is thine eye. Wherefore if thine eye be single, all thy body shall be full of light. But and if thine

---

[1] 1525 version: . . . and reconcile thyself to thy brother . . .

eye be wicked then all thy body shall be full of darkness.[1]
Wherefore if the light that is in thee, be darkness: how
great is that darkness.

No man can serve two masters. For either he shall hate
the one and love the other: or else he shall lean to the one
and despise the other: ye can not serve God and mammon.
Therefore I say unto you, be not careful for your life, what
ye shall eat, or what ye shall drink, nor yet for your body,
what ye shall put on. Is not the life more worth than meat,
and the body more of value that raiment? Behold the fowls
of the air: for they sow not, neither reap, nor yet carry in to
the barns: and yet your heavenly father feedeth them. Are
ye not much better than they?

Which of you (though he took thought therefore) could
put one cubit unto his stature? And why care ye then for
raiment? Consider the lilies of the field,[2] how they grow.
They labour not neither spin. And yet for all that I say unto
you, that even Solomon in all his royalty was not arrayed
like unto one of these.

Wherefore if God so clothe the grass, which is today in
the field, and tomorrow shall be cast into the furnace: shall
he not much more do the same unto you, o ye of little faith?

Therefore take no thought saying: what shall we eat, or
what shall we drink, or wherewith shall we be clothed?
After all these things seek the gentiles. For your heavenly
father knoweth that ye have need of all these things. But
rather seek ye first the kingdom of heaven and the righteousness thereof, and all these things shall be ministered unto you.

Care not then for the morrow, but let the morrow care
for itself: for the day present hath every enough of his own
trouble.

[1] 1525 version: . . . is full of light . . . then is all thy body full of
darkness.
[2] 1525 version: Behold the lilies of the field . . .

Matthew VIII. 28–34

And when he was come to the other side, in to the country of the Gergesites, there met him two possessed of devils, which came out of the graves, and were out of measure fierce, so that no man might go by that way. And behold they cried out saying: O Jesu the son of God, what have we to do with thee? Art thou come hither to torment us before the time be come? And there was a good way off from them a great herd of swine feeding. Then the devils besought him saying: if thou cast us out, suffer us to go our way into the herd of swine. And he said unto them: go your ways. Then went they out, and departed into the herd of swine. And behold the whole herd of swine was carried with violence headlong[1] into the sea, and perished in the water. Then the herdsmen fled and went their ways into the city, and told everything, and what had fortuned unto the possessed of the devils. And behold all the city came out and met Jesus. And when they saw him, they besought him to depart out of their coasts.

Matthew XXVII. 35–53

When they had crucified him, they parted his garments, and did cast lots: to fulfil that was spoken by the prophet. They divided my garments among them: and upon my vesture did cast lots. And they sat and watched him there. And they set up over his head the cause of his death written. This is Jesus the king of the Jews. And there were two thieves crucified with him, one on the right hand, and another on the left.

[1] Tyndale writes 'hedlinge', an earlier word meaning the same as 'headlong'; its latest recorded use was in 1603. The first two occurrences of 'headlong' are in 1482 and 1548.

Tyndale (1534)

They that passed by, reviled him wagging their heads and saying: Thou that destroyest the temple of God and buildest it in three days, save thyself. If thou be the son of God, come down from the cross. Likewise also the high priests mocking him with the scribes and elders said: He saved other, himself he can not save. If he be the king of Israel: let him now come down from the cross, and we will believe him. He trusted in God, let him deliver him now, if he will have him: for he said, I am the son of God. That same also the thieves which were crucified with him, cast in his teeth.

From the sixth hour was there darkness over all the land unto the ninth hour. And about the ninth hour Jesus cried with a loud voice, saying: Eli Eli lama sabathani. That is to say, my God, my God, why has thou forsaken me? Some of them that stood there, when they heard that, said: This man calleth for Helyas. And straight way one of them ran and took a sponge and filled it full of vinegar, and put it on a reed, and gave him to drink. Other said, let be: let us see whether Helyas will come and deliver him. Jesus cried again with a loud voice and yielded up the ghost.

And behold the veil of the temple did rent in twain from the top to the bottom, and the earth did quake, and the stones did rent, and graves did open: and the bodies of many saints which slept, arose and came out of the graves after his resurrection, and came into the holy city, and appeared unto many.

Luke XXI. 20–28

And when ye see Jerusalem besieged with a host, then understand that the desolation of the same is nigh. Then let them which are in Iewrye fly to the mountains. And let them which are in the midst of it, depart out. And let not

47

them that are in other countries, enter there in. For these be the days of vengeance, to fulfil all that are written. But woe be to them that be with child, and to them that give suck in those days: for there shall be great trouble in the land, and wrath over all this people. And they shall fall on the edge of the sword, and shall be led captive, into all nations. And Jerusalem shall be trodden under foot of the gentiles, until the time of the gentiles be fulfilled.

And there shall be signs in the sun, and in the moon, and in the stars: and in the earth the people shall be in such perplexity, that they shall not tell which way to turn themselves. The sea and the waters shall roar,[1] and mens hearts shall fail them for fear, and for looking after those things which shall come on the earth. For the powers of heaven shall move. And then shall they see the son of man come in a cloud with power and great glory. When these things begin to come to pass: then look up, and lift up your heads for your redemption draweth nigh.

Romans XIII. 7–14

Give to every man therefore his duty: Tribute to whom tribute belongeth: Custom to whom custom is due: fear to whom fear belongeth: Honour to whom honour pertaineth. Owe nothing to any man: but to love one another. 'For he that loveth another, fulfilleth the law. For these commandments: Thou shalt not commit adultery: Thou shalt not kill: Thou shalt not steal: Thou shalt not bear false witness: Thou shalt not desire and so forth (if there be any other commandment) they are all comprehended in this saying: Love thine neighbour as thy self. Love hurteth not his neighbour. Therefore is love the fulfilling of the law.

[1] 1525 version: The sea and the waves shall roar . . .

Tyndale (1534)

This also we know, I mean the season, how that it is time that we should now awake out of sleep. For now is our salvation nearer than when we believed. The night is passed and the day is come nigh. Let us therefore cast away the deeds of darkness, and let us put on the Armour of light. Let us walk honestly as it were in the day light: not in eating and drinking: neither in chambering and wantonness: neither in strife and envying: but put ye on the Lord Jesus Christ. And make not provision for the flesh, to fulfil the lusts of it.

The Epistle of Ash Wednesday Joel II. 12–19

And now therefore sayeth the lord. Turn to me with all your hearts, in fasting and lamentation. And tear your hearts and not your garments, and turn unto the lord your God. For he is full of mercy and compassion, long ere he be angry, and great in mercy and repenteth when he is at the point to punish. Who can tell whether the lord will turn and have compassion and shall leave after him a blessing? Sacrifice and drink offering unto the lord your God. Blow a trumpet in Sion, proclaim fasting and call a congregation. Gather the people together, bring the elders to one place, gather the young children and they that suck the breasts, together. Let the bridegroom come out of his chamber and the bride out of her parlour. Let the priests that minister unto the lord, weep between the porch and the altar, and say: spare (lord) thy people and deliver not thine inheritance unto rebuke that the heathen should reign over them. Why should they say: among the nations, where is their god. And the lord envied for his lands sake and had compassion on his people. And the lord answered and said unto his people Behold, I sent you corn, new wine and oil, that ye shall be

49

satisfied therewith. Neither will I deliver you any more unto the heathen.

The Epistle of St Katherine's Day   *Ecclesiasticus* LI. 13–17

Lord, I did lift up my prayer upon the earth, and besought to be delivered from death. I called upon the lord the father of my lord, that he should not leave me helpless in the day of my tribulation, and in the day of the proud man. I praised thy name perpetually, and honoured it with confession, and my prayer was heard. And thou savedst me that I perished not, and deliveredest me out of the time of unrighteousness: Therefore will I confess and praise thee, and will bless the name of the Lord.

2

COVERDALE (1535)

Coverdale's complete Bible, a large blackletter folio first issued in 1535 at Cologne, was the first ever to be printed in English. He translated from German, apparently from the Swiss German adaptation of Luther's Bible printed at Zürich in 1531, and a Dominican Latin version of 1582. He was a friend of Tyndale and had worked with that master, but he was not then a young man. A second edition of this first Coverdale Bible appeared in London in 1537, without substantial changes. It will be seen that Coverdale had worked fast, and his first Bible was in fact soon superseded both by others and by his own later work, but the 1535 Bible cannot be dismissed as hasty or immature, and it is more purely his own than what he did afterwards.

The Prophet Esay (*Isaiah*) LI

Harken unto me, ye that hold of righteousness, ye that seek the LORD. Take heed unto the stone, whereout ye are hewen, and to the grave whereout ye are digged. Consider Abraham your father, and Sarah that bare you: how that I called him alone, prospered him well, and increased him: how the LORD comforted Sion, and repaired all her decay: making her desert as a paradise, and her wilderness as the garden of the LORD. Mirth and joy was there, thanksgiving and your voice of praise. Have respect unto me then (o my people) and lay thine ear to me: for a law, and an ordinance shall go forth from me, to lighten the Gentiles. It is hard by, that my health and my righteousness shall go forth, and the people shall be ordered with mine arm.

The Islands (that is the Gentiles) shall hope in me, and put their trust in mine arm. Lift up your eyes toward heaven, and look upon the earth beneath. For the heavens shall vanish away like smoke, and the earth shall tear like a cloth, and they that dwell therein, shall perish in like manner. But my health endureth for ever, and my righteousness shall not cease. Therefore harken unto me, ye that have pleasure in righteousness, thou people that bearest my law in thine heart. Fear not the curse of men, be not afraid of their blasphemies and revilings: for worms and moths shall eat them up like cloth and wool. But my righteousness shall endure for ever, and my saving health from generation to generation.

Wake up, wake up, and be strong: O thou arm of the LORD: wake up, like as in times past, ever and since the world began. Art not thou he that hast wounded that proud lucifer, and hewen the dragon in pieces? Art not thou even he, which hast dried up the deep of the sea, which hast made plain the sea ground, that the delivered might go through? That the redeemed of the LORD, which turned again, might come with joy unto Sion, there to endure for ever. That mirth and gladness might be with them: that sorrow and woe might flee from them. Yea I, I am even he, that in all things giveth you consolation. What art thou then, that fearest a mortal man, ye child of man, which goeth away as doth the flower? And forgettest the LORD that made thee, that spread out the heavens, and laid the foundation of the earth. But thou art ever afraid for the sight of thine oppressor, which is ready to do harm: Where is the wrath of the oppressor? It cometh on fast, it maketh haste to appear: It shall not perish, that it should not be able to destroy, neither shall it fail for fault of nourishing. I am the LORD God, that make the sea to be still, and to rage: whose name is the LORD of hosts. I shall put my word also in thy mouth, and defend thee with the turning of my hand that thou mayest plant the heavens, and lay the foundations of the earth, and say unto Sion: thou art my people.

Awake, Awake, and stand up o Jerusalem, thou that from the hand of the LORD hast drunk out of the cup of his wrath thou that hast supped of, and sucked out the slumbering cup to the bottom. For among all the sons whom thou hast begotten there is not one that may hold thee up: and not one to lead thee by the hand, of all the sons that thou hast nourished. Both these things are happened unto thee, but who is sorry for it? Yea, destruction, wasting, hunger and sword: but who hath comforted thee? Thy sons lie comfortless at the head of every street like a taken venison, and are full of the terrible wrath of the LORD, and punishment of thy God. And therefore thou miserable and drunk (howbeit not with wine) hear this: Thus sayeth thy LORD: thy LORD and God, the defender of his people: Behold, I will take the slumbering cup out of thy hand, even the cup of the dregs of my wrath: that from hence forth thou shalt never drink it more, and will put it in their hand that trouble thee: which have spoken to thy soul: stoop down, that we may go over thee: make thy body even with the ground, and as the street to go upon.

The Prophet Esay (*Isaiah*) LX

And therefore get thee up by times, for thy light cometh, and the glory of the LORD shall rise up upon thee. For lo, while the darkness and cloud covereth the earth and the people, the LORD shall show thee light, and his glory shall be seen in thee. The Gentiles shall come to thy light, and Kings to the brightness that springeth forth upon thee. Lift up thine eyes, and look round about thee: All these gather themselves, and come to thee. Sons shall come unto thee from far, and daughters shall gather themselves to thee on every side. When thou seest this, thou shalt marvel exceedingly, and thine heart shall be opened: when the power of the sea shall be converted unto thee (that is) when the strength of the Gentiles shall come unto thee. The multitude of Camels shall cover thee, the dromedaries of Madian and Epha. All they of Saba shall come, bringing gold and incense and showing the praise of the LORD. All the cattle of Cedar shall be gathered unto ye, the rams of Nabaioth shall serve thee, to be offered upon mine altar, which I have chosen, and in the house of my glory which I have furnished. But what are these that flee here like the clouds, and as the doves flying to their windows?

The Isles also shall gather them unto me, and specially the ships of the sea: that they may bring thee sons from far, and their silver and their gold with them, unto the name of the LORD thy God, unto the holy one of Israel, that hath glorified thee. Strangers shall build up thy walls, and their kings shall do thee service. For when I am angry, I smite thee: and when it pleaseth me, I pardon thee. Thy gates shall stand open still both day and night, and never be shut: that the host of the Gentiles may come, and that their kings may be brought unto thee. For every people and kingdom that serveth not thee, shall perish, and be destroyed with the sword. The glory of Libanus shall come unto thee: The Fir trees, Boxes and Cedars together, to garnish the place of my Sanctuary, for I will glorify the place of my feet.

Moreover those shall come kneeling unto thee, that have vexed thee: and all they that despised thee, shall fall down at thy feet. Thou shalt be called the city of the LORD, the holy Sion of Israel. Because thou hast been forsaken and hated, so that no man went through thee: I will make thee glorious for ever and ever, and joyful throughout all posterities. Thou shalt suck the milk of the Gentiles, and kings' breasts shall feed thee. And thou shalt know that I the LORD am thy Saviour and defender, the mighty one of Jacob. For brass will I give thee gold, and for iron silver, for wood brass, and for stones iron. I will make peace thy ruler, and righteousness thine officer. Violence and robbery shall never be heard of in thy land, neither harm and destruction within thy borders. Thy walls shall be called health, and thy gates the praise of God. The Sun shall never be thy daylight, and the light of the Moon shall never shine unto thee: but the LORD himself shall be thy everlasting light, and thy God shall be thy glory.

Thy sun shall never go down, and thy Moon shall not be taken away, for the LORD himself shall be thy everlasting light, and thy sorrowful days shall be rewarded thee. Thy people shall be all godly, and possess the land for ever: the flower of my planting, the work of my hands, whereof I will rejoice. The youngest and least shall grow into a thousand, and the simplest into a strong people. I the LORD shall shortly bring this thing to pass in his time.

Micheas (Micah) 1

This is the word of the LORD, that came unto Micheas the Morastite, in the days of Joathan, Achas, and Ezechias kings of Judah: which was shown him upon Samaria and Jerusalem.

Hear all ye people, mark this well o earth, and all that therein is: yea the LORD God himself be witness among you, even ye LORD from his holy temple. For why? behold, the LORD shall go out of his place, and come down, and tread upon the high things of the earth. The mountains shall consume under him, and the valleys shall cleave asunder: like as wax consumeth at the fire, and as the waters run downward. And all this shall be for the wickedness of Jacob, and the sins of the house of Israel.

But what is the wickedness of Jacob? Is not Samaria? Which are the high places of Juda? Is not Jerusalem? Therefore I shall make Samaria an heap of stones in the field, to lay about the vineyard: her stones shall I cast into the valley, and discover her foundations. All her images shall be broken down and all her winnings shall be burnt in the fire: yea all her idols will I destroy: for why, they are gathered out of the hire of an whore, and into an whore's hire shall they be turned again. Wherefore I will mourn and make lamentation, bare and naked will I go: I must mourn like the dragons, and take sorrow as the ostriches: for their wound is past remedy: And why? it is come in to Juda, and hath touched the port[1] of my people at Jerusalem already. Weep not, lest they at Geth perceive it.

Thou at Betaphra, welter thyself in the dust and ashes. Thou that dwellest at Sephir, get thee hence with shame. The proud shall boast no more for ever sorrow: and why? her neighbour shall take from her what she hath. The rebellious city hopeth, that it shall not be so evil: but for all that, the snare[2] shall come from the LORD, even into the

[1] 'Port' means a gate or door.
[2] Where I have written 'snare' Coverdale has 'plage'; it certainly means 'snare' in Chapter 2; it is a rare word otherwise attested apparently only in 1608, but it also occurs as a spelling of 'plague' and there might be some confusion. In chapter 5 'he plageth them' must mean 'he plagues them'.

port of Jerusalem. The great noise of the chariots[1] shall fear
them, that dwell at Lachis, which is an occasion of the sin
of the daughter of Sion, for in thee came up the wickedness
of Israel. Yea she sent her coursers in to the land of Geth.

The houses of lies will deceive the kings of Israel. And as
for thee (o thou that dwellest at Morassa) I shall bring a
possessioner upon thee, and the snare of Israel shall reach
unto Odolla. Make thee bald, and shave thee, because of
thy tender children: Make thee clean bald as an Eagle, for
they shall be carried away captive from thee.

Micheas 11

Woe unto them, that imagine to do harm, and devise
ungraciousness upon their beds, to perform it in the clear
day: for their power is against God. When they covet to
have land, they take it by violence, they rob men of their
houses.

Thus they oppress a man for his house, and every man
for his heritage. Therefore thus sayeth the LORD: Behold,
against this household have I devised a snare, whereout ye
shall not pluck your necks: ye shall no more go so proudly,
for it will be a perilous time. In that day shall this term be
used, and a mourning shall be made over you on this
manner: We be utterly desolate, the portion of my people is
translated. When will he part unto us the land, that he hath
taken from us?

Nevertheless there shall be no man to divide thee thy
portion, in the congregation of the LORD. Tush, hold your
tongue (say they). It shall not fall upon this people, we shall
not come so to confusion, sayeth the house of Jacob. Is the
spirit of the LORD so clean away? or is he so minded? Truth
it is, my words are friendly unto them that live right: but

[1] Coverdale writes 'charettes' where I have put 'chariots'.

my people doth the contrary, therefore must I take part against them: for they take away both coat and cloak from the simple.

Ye have turned yourselves to fight, the women of my people have ye shut out from their good houses, and taken away my excellent gifts from their children. Up, get you hence, for here shall ye have no rest.

Because of their idolatry they are corrupt, and shall miserably perish. If I were a fleshly fellow, and a preacher of lies and told them that they might sit bibbing and bowling, and be drunken: O that were a prophet for this people.

But I will gather thee indeed (o Jacob) and drive the remnant of Israel all together. I shall carry them one with another, as a flock in the fold, and as the cattle in their stalls, that they may be disquieted of other men.

Who so breaketh the gap, he shall go before. They shall break up the port, and go in and out at it. Their king shall go before them, and the LORD shall be upon the head of them.

Micheas III

Hear, o ye heads of the house of Jacob, and ye leaders of the house of Israel: Should not ye know, what were lawful and right? But ye hate the good, and love the evil: ye pluck off mens skins, and the flesh from their bones: ye eat the flesh of my people, and flay off their skin: ye break their bones, ye chop them in pieces as it were into a cauldron, and as flesh into a pot. Now the time shall come, that when they call unto the LORD, he shall not hear them, but hide his face from them: because that through their own imagination, they have dealt so wickedly.

And as concerning the prophets that deceive my people, thus the LORD sayeth against them: When they have anything to bite upon, then they preach that all shall be well: but if a man put not something into their mouths, they preach of war against him.

Therefore your vision shall be turned to night, and your prophesying to darkness. The sun shall go down over those prophets, and the day shall be dark unto them. Then shall the vision seers be ashamed, and the soothsayers confounded: yea they shall be fain (all the pack of them) to stop their mouths, for they have not Gods word. As for me, I am full of strength, and of the spirit of the LORD, full of judgement and boldness: to show the house of Jacob their wickedness, and the house of Israel their sin.

O hear this ye rulers of the house of Jacob, and ye judges of the house of Israel: ye that abhor the thing that is lawful, and wrest aside the thing that is straight: ye that build up Sion with blood, and Jerusalem with doing wrong. O ye judges, ye give sentence for gifts: O ye priests, ye teach for lucre: O ye prophets, ye prophecy for money. Yet will they be taken as those that hold upon God, and say: Is not the LORD among us? Tush, there can no misfortune happen us. Therefore shall Sion (for your sakes) be ploughed like a field: Jerusalem shall become an heap of stones, and the hill of ye temple shall be turned to an high wood.

Micheas IV

But in the latter days it will come to pass, that the hill of the LORDS house shall be set up higher than any mountains or hills: Yea the people shall praise unto it, and the multitude of the Gentiles shall haste them hither, saying: Come, let us go up to the hill of the LORD, and to the house of the God of Jacob: that he may teach us his way, and that we may walk in his paths.

For the law shall come out of Sion, and the word of God from Jerusalem, and shall give sentence among the multitude of the heathen, and reform the people of far countries: so that of their swords they shall make ploughshares, and scythes of their spears.

One people shall not lift up a sword against another, yea they shall no more learn to fight: but every man shall sit under his vineyard and under his fig tree, and no man to fray him away: for the mouth of the LORD of hosts hath spoken it. Therefore, whereas all people have walked every man in the name of his own god, we will walk in the name of our God forever and ever. At the same time (sayeth the LORD) will I gather up the lame and the outcasts, and such as I have chastened: and will give issue unto the lame, and make of ye outcasts a great people: and the LORD himself shall be their king upon the mount Sion, from this time forth for evermore. And unto thee (O thou tower of Eder, thou stronghold of the daughter Sion) unto thee shall it come: even the first lordship and kingdom of the daughter Jerusalem. Why then art thou now so heavy? Is there no king in thee? Are thy counsellors away that thou art so pained, as a woman in her travail?

And now (o thou daughter Sion) be sorry, let it grieve thee as a wife labouring with child: for now must thou get thee out of the city, and dwell upon the plain field: Yea unto Babilon shalt thou go, there shalt thou be delivered, and there the LORD shall loose thee from the hand of thine enemies.

Now also are there many people gathered together against thee, saying: what, Sion is cursed, we shall see our lust upon her. But they know not the thoughts of the LORD, they understand not his counsel, that shall gather them together as the sheaves in the barn. Therefore get thee up (o thou daughter Sion) and thrash out the corn. For I will make thy horn iron, and thy claws brass, that thou mayest grind many people: their goods shall thou appropriate unto the LORD, and their substance into the ruler of the whole world.

Micheas v

After that shalt thou be robbed thyself, o thou robbers daughter: they shall lay siege against us, and smite the judge of Israel with a rod upon the cheek. And thou Bethleem Ephrata, art little among the thousands of Juda, Out of thee shall come one unto me, which shall be the governor in Israel: whose outgoing hath been from the beginning, and from everlasting. In the meanwhile he plagueth them for a season, until the time that she (which shall bear) have born: then shall the remnant of his brethren be converted unto the children of Israel. He shall stand fast, and give food in the strength of the LORD, and in the victory of the name of the LORD his God: and when they be converted, he shall be magnified unto the farthest parts of the world.

Then shall there be peace, so that the Assirian may come in to our land, and tread in our houses. We shall bring up seven shepherds and eight princes upon them: these shall subdue the land of Assur with the sword, and the land of Nymrod with their naked weapons. Thus shall he deliver us from the Assirian, when he cometh within our land, and setteth his foot within our borders. And the remnant of Jacob shall be among the multitude of people, as the dew of the LORD, and as the drops upon the grass, that tarrieth for no man, and waiteth of nobody. Yea the residue of Jacob shall be among the Gentiles and the multitude of people, as the lion among the beasts of the wood, and as the lions whelp among a flock of sheep: which (when he goeth through) treadeth down, teareth in pieces, and there is no man that can help. Thine hand shall be lift up upon thine enemies, and all thine adversaries shall perish.

The time shall come also (sayeth the LORD) that I will take thine horses from thee, and destroy thy chariots. I will break down the cities of thy land, and overthrow all thy strongholds. All witchcrafts will I root out of thine hand, there shall no more soothsayings be within thee. Thine Idols and thine images will I destroy out of thee so that thou shalt no more bow thyself unto the works of thine own hands. Thy groves will I pluck up by the roots, and break down thy cities. Thus will I be avenged also, upon all heathen that will not hear.

Micheas VI

Harken now what the LORD sayeth: Up, reprove the mountains, and let the hills hear thy voice. O hear the punishment of the LORD, ye mountains, and ye mighty foundations of the earth: for the LORD will reprove his people, and reason with Israel: O my people, what have I done unto thee? or wherein have I hurt thee? give me answer. Because I brought thee from the land of Egypt, and delivered thee out of the house of bondage? Because I made Moses, Aaron and Miriam to lead thee? Remember (o my people) what Balach the king of Moab had imagined against thee, and what answer that Balaam the son of Beor gave him, from Sethim unto Galgal: that ye may know the loving kindness of the LORD.

What acceptable thing shall I offer unto the LORD? shall I bow my knee to the high God? Shall I come before him with burnt offerings, and with calves of a year old? Hath the LORD a pleasure in many thousand rams, or innumerable streams of oil? Or shall I give my first born for mine offences, and the fruit of my body for the sin of my soule? I will show thee (O man) what is good, and what the LORD requireth of thee: Namely, to do right, to have pleasure in loving kindness, to be lowly, and to walk with thy God: that thou mayest be called a city of the LORD, and that thy name may be righteousness. Hear (o ye tribes) who would else give you such warning? Should I not be displeased, for the unrighteous good[1] in the houses of the wicked, and because the measure is minished? Or should I justify the false balances and the bag of deceitful weights, among those that be full of riches unrighteously gotten: where the citizens deal with falsety, speak lies, and have deceitful tongues in their mouths.

Therefore I will take in hand to punish thee, and to make thee desolate, because of thy sins. Thou shalt eat, and not have enough: yea thou shalt bring thyself down. Thou shalt flee, but not escape: and those that thou wouldst save, will I deliver to the sword. Thou shalt sow, but not reap: thou shalt press out olives, but oil shalt thou not have, to annoint thyself withal: thou shalt tread out sweet must, but shalt drink no wine. Ye keep the ordinances of Amri, and all the customs of the house of Achab: ye follow their pleasures, therefore will I make thee waste, and cause the inhabiters to be abhorred, O my people; and thus shalt thou bear thine own shame.

Micheas VII

Woe is me: I am become as one, that goeth a gleaning in the harvest. There are no more grapes to eat, yet would I fain (with all my heart) have of the best fruit. There is not a

[1] 'Good' is here used as a verb, meaning 'doing well'; the usage is Old English, and was infrequent, but it survived the sixteenth century.

godly man upon earth, there is not one righteous among men. They labour all to shed blood, and every man hunteth his brother to death: yet they say they do well, when they do evil. As the prince will, so sayeth the judge: that he may do him a pleasure again. The great man speaketh what his heart desireth, and the hearers allow him. The best of them is but as a thistle, and the most righteous of them is but as a brier in the hedge. But when the day of thy preachers cometh, that thou shalt be visited: then shall they be wasted away. Let no man believe his friend, nor put his confidence in a prince. Keep the port of thy mouth, from her that lyeth in thy bosom: for the son shall put his father to dishonour, the daughter shall rise against her mother, the daughter-in-law against her mother-in-law: and a mans foes shall be even they of his own household.

Nevertheless I will look up unto the LORD, I will patiently abide God my saviour: my God shall hear me. O thou enemy of mine, rejoice not at my fall, for I shall get up again: and though I sit in darkness, yet the LORD is my light. I will bear the punishment of the LORD (for why, I have offended him) till he sit in judgement upon my cause, and see that I have right. He will bring me forth to the light, and I shall see his righteousness.

She that is mine enemy shall look upon it, and be confounded, which now sayeth: Where is thy LORD God? Mine eyes shall behold her, when she shall be trodden down, as the clay in the streets. The time will come, that thy gaps shall be made up, and the law shall go abroad: and at that time shall they come unto thee, from Assur unto the strong cities, and from the strong cities unto the river: from the one sea to the other, from the one mountain to the other.

Notwithstanding the land must be wasted, because of them that dwell therein, and for the fruits of their own imaginations. Therefore feed thy people with thy rod, the flock of thine heritage which dwell desolate in the wood: that they may be fed upon the mount of Charmel, Basan and Galaad as aforetime. Marvellous things will I show them, like as when they came out of Egypt. This shall the heathen see, and be ashamed for all their power: so that they shall lay their hand upon their mouth, and stop their ears. They shall lick the dust like a serpent, and as the worms of the earth, that tremble in their holes. They shall be afraid of the LORD our God, and they shall fear thee.

Where is there such a God as thou? that pardon wickedness, and forgivest the offences of the remnant of thine heritage? He keepeth not his wrath for ever. And with thee his delight is to have compassion: he shall turn again, and be merciful to us: he shall put down our wickednesses, and cast all our sins into the bottom of the sea. Thou shalt keep thy trust with Jacob, and thy mercy for Abraham, like as thou hast sworn unto our fathers long ago.

John VI

After this went Jesus over the sea unto the city Tiberias in Galilee. And much people followed him, because they saw the tokens that he did upon them which were diseased. But Jesus went up in to a mountain, and there he sat with his disciples. And Easter the feast of the Jews was nigh. Then Jesus lift up his eyes, and saw that there came much people unto him, and he said unto Philip: Whence shall we buy bread, that these may eat? But this he said to prove him, for he himself knew, what he would do.

Philip answered him: Two hundred penny worth of bread is not enough among them, that every one may take a little. Then said unto him one of his disciples, Andrew the brother of Simon Peter: There is a lad here, that hath five barley loaves, and two fishes, but what is that among so many? Jesus said: Make the people sit down. There was much grass in the place. Then they sat them down, about a five thousand men. Jesus took the loaves, thanked, and gave them to the disciples: the disciples (gave) to them that were set down. Likewise also of the fishes as much as they would.

When they were filled, he said unto his disciples: Gather up the broken meat that remaineth, that nothing be lost. Then they gathered, and filled twelve baskets with the broken meat, that remained of the five barley loaves, unto them which had eaten. Now when the men saw the token that Jesus did, they said: This is of a truth the Prophet, that should come into the world. When Jesus now perceived that they would come, and take him up, to make him king, he gat him away again into a mountain himself alone.

At even went his disciples down to the sea, and entered into the ship, and came to the other side of the sea unto Capernaum. And it was dark already. And Jesus was not come to them. And the sea arose through a great wind. Now when they had rowed upon a five and twenty or thirty furlongs, they saw Jesus going upon the sea, and came nigh to the ship. And they were afraid. But he said unto them: It is I, be not afraid. Then would they have received him into the ship. And immediately the ship was at the land whither they went.

The next day after, the people which stood on the other side of the sea, saw that there was none other ship there save that one, wherein to his disciples were entered: and that Jesus went not in with his disciples into the ship, but that his disciples were gone away alone. Howbeit there came other ships from Tiberias, nigh unto the place where they had eaten the bread, after that the LORD had given thanks.

Now when the people saw that Jesus was not there, neither his disciples, they took ship also, and came to Capernaum, and sought Jesus.

And when they found him on the other side of the sea, they said unto him: Master, when camest thou hither? Jesus answered them, and said: Verily verily I say unto you: ye seek me not because ye saw the tokens, but because ye ate of the loaves, and were filled. Labour not for the meat which perisheth but that endureth unto everlasting life, which the son of man shall give you: for him hath God the father sealed.

Then said they unto him: What shall we do, that we may work the works of God? Jesus answered, and said unto them: This is the work of God, that ye believe on him, whom he hath sent. Then said they unto him: What token dost thou then, that we may see and believe thee? What workest thou? Our fathers ate Manna in the wilderness, as it is written: he gave them bread from heaven to eat. Then said Jesus unto them: Verily verily I say unto you: Moses gave you not bread from heaven, but my father gaveth you the true bread from heaven: for this is that bread of God, which cometh from heaven, and giveth life unto the world.

Then said they unto him: Sir, give us always such bread. But Jesus said unto them: I am that bread of life. He that cometh unto me, shall not hunger: and he that believeth on me, shall never thirst. But I have said unto you, that ye have seen me, and yet ye believe not. All that my father giveth me, cometh unto me: and whoso cometh unto me, him will not I cast out: for I am come down from heaven, not to do mine own will, but the will of him that hath sent me.

This is the will of the father which hath sent me, that of all that he hath given me, I should lose nothing, but should raise it up again at the last day. This is the will of him which hath sent me, that, whosoever seeth the son and believeth on him, have everlasting life, and I shall raise him up at the last day.

Then murmured the Jews thereover, that he said: I am that bread which is come down from heaven, and they said: Is not this Jesus, Joseph's son, whose father and mother we know? How sayeth he then, I am come down from heaven? Jesus answered, and said unto them: Murmur not among yourselves. No man can come unto me, except the father which hath sent me, draw him. And I shall raise him up at the last day. It is written in the prophets: They shall all be taught of God. Whosoever now heareth it of the father, and learneth it, cometh unto me. Not that any man hath seen the father, save he which is of the father, the same hath seen the father.

Verily verily I say unto you: he that believeth in me, hath everlasting life. I am that bread of life. Your fathers ate Manna in the wilderness, and are dead. This is that bread which cometh from heaven, that who so eateth thereof, should not die. I am that living bread, which come down from heaven: Who so eateth of this bread, shall live for ever. And the bread that I will give, is my flesh which I will give for the life of the world.

Then strove the Jews among themselves, and said: how can this fellow give us his flesh to eat? Jesus said unto them: Verily, verily I say unto you: Except ye eat the flesh of the son of man and drink his blood, ye have no life in you. Whoso eateth my flesh, and drinketh my blood, have everlasting life: and I shall raise him up at the last day. For my flesh is the very meat, and my blood is the very drink. Whoso eateth my flesh, and drinketh my blood, abideth in me, and I in him. As the living father hath sent me, and I live for the fathers sake: Even so he that eateth me, shall live for my sake. This is the bread which is come from heaven:

Not as your fathers ate Manna, and are dead. He that eateth of this bread, shall live for ever.

These things said he in the synagogue, when he taught at Capernaum. Many now of his disciples that heard this, said: This is an hard saying, who may abide the hearing of it? But when Jesus perceived in himself, that his disciples murmured thereat he said unto them: Doth this offend you? What and if ye shall see the son of man ascend up thither, where he was afore. It is the spirit that quickeneth, the flesh profiteth nothing. The words that I speak, are spirit, and are life. But there are some among you, that believe not For Jesus knew well from the beginning, which they were that believed not, and who should betray him. And he said: Therefore have I said unto you: No man can come unto me, except it be given him of my father.

From that time forth, many of his disciples went back, and walked no more with him. Then said Jesus unto the twelve: Will ye also go away? Then answered Simon Peter: LORD, Whither shall we go? Thou hast the words of everlasting life: and we have believed and known, that thou art Christ the son of the living God. Jesus answered them. Have I not chosen you twelve, and one of you is a devil? But he spake of Judas Simon Iscarioth: the same betrayed him afterward, and was one of the twelve.

3

MATTHEW'S BIBLE (1537)

This Bible was the first to be printed in England: it was compounded from the unpublished papers of Tyndale and the published work of Coverdale, by John Rogers, a friend and colleague of Tyndale, with some use of French Bibles of 1534 and 1535; it was issued under the pseudonym of Thomas Matthew in 1537 in London. Substantially it belonged to Tyndale, who was martyred in 1536; it became extremely popular in England. But the posthumous appearance of the work of Tyndale was the end of a chapter; the age of episcopal committees was now to begin, and the pressure under which official Bibles were produced would inevitably be of a different kind. Matthew's Bible did not survive long in official favour; John Rogers was not employed on later biblical translation and was burned to death in 1555.

Genesis XLIX. 1–28

And Jacob called for his sons and said: come together, that I may tell you what shall happen you in the last days. Gather you together and hear ye sons of Jacob and harken unto Israel your father.

Ruben thou art mine eldest son, my might and the beginning of my strength, chief in receiving and chief in power.

As unstable as water wast thou: thou shalt therefore not be the chiefest, for thou went up upon thy fathers bed, and then defiledest thou my couch with going up.

The brethren Simon and Levi, wicked instruments are their weapons. Into their secrets come not my soul, and unto their congregation be my honour not coupled: for in their wrath they slew a man, and in their self will they houghed[1] an ox. Cursed be their wrath for it was strong, and their fierceness for it was cruel. I will therefore divide them in Jacob, and scatter them in Israel.

Juda, thy brethren shall praise thee, and thine hand shall be in the neck of thine enemies, and thy fathers children shall stoop unto thee. Juda is a lions whelp, from spoil my son thou art come on high: he laid him down and couched himself as a lion, and as a lioness. Who dare stir him up? The sceptre shall not depart from Juda, nor a ruler from between his legs until Sylo come, unto whom the people shall harken. He shall bind his foal unto the vine, and his asses colt unto the vine branch, and shall wash his garment in wine and his mantle in the blood of grapes, his eyes are ruddier than wine, and his teeth whiter than milk.

Zabulon shall dwell in the haven of the sea and in the port of ships, and shall reach unto Sydon.

Isachar is a strong ass, he couched him down between two borders, and saw that rest was good and the land that it was pleasant, and bowed his shoulder to bear, and became a servant unto tribute. Dan shall judge his people, as one of the tribes of Israel. Dan shall be a serpent in the way, and an adder in the path, and bite the horses heels, so that his rider shall fall backward. After thy saving look I lord.

Gad, men of war shall invade him. And he shall turn them to flight.

---

[1] To 'hough' is to hamstring; the word was in use in standard English as late as 1878.

Of Asser cometh fat breed, and he shall give pleasures for a king.

Nepthalim is a swift hind, and giveth goodly words. That flourishing child Joseph, that flourishing child and goodly unto the eye: the daughters ran upon the wall. The shooters have envied him and chid with him and hated him, and yet his bow bowed fast, and his arms and his hands were strong, by the hands of the mighty God of Jacob: out of him shall come an hard man a stone in Israel. Thy fathers god shall help thee, and the almighty shall bless thee with blessings from heaven above, and with blessings of the water that lieth under, and with blessings of the breasts and of the womb. The blessings of thy father were strong: even as the blessings of my elders, after the desire of the highest in the world, and these blessings shall fall on the head of Joseph, and on the top of the head of him that was separate from his brethren.

Benjamin is a ravishing wolf. In the morning he shall devour his prey, and at night he shall divide his spoil.

All these are the twelve tribes of Israel, and this is that which their father spake unto them.

1 Samuel c. XXVI

After that came the Ziphites unto Saul to Gabaah saying: David hideth himself in the hill of Hachilah even before the wilderness. Then Saul arose and went to the wilderness of Ziph and three thousand chosen men of Israel with him, for to seek David in the wilderness of Ziph. And Saul pitched in the hill of Hachilah which lieth before the wilderness, by the way's side. But David dwelt in the wilderness. And when he saw that Saul came after him into the wilderness, he sent out spies and understood that Saul was come of surety.

Wherefore David arose and went to the place where Saul had pitched, and beheld the place where Saul lay with Abner the son of Ner his chief captain. For Saul lay within a round bank, and the people pitched round about him. Then answered David and spake to Ahimelech the Hethite and to Abisai the son of Zaruiah and brother to Joab saying: who will go down with me to Saul to the host? and Abisai said: I will go down with thee.

And so David and Abisai came to ye people by night. And behold, Saul lay sleeping within a round bank and his spear pitched in the ground at his head, Abner and the people lying round about him. Then said Abisai to David: God hath closed in thine enemy unto thine hand this day. Now therefore let me smite him a fellowship with my spear to ye earth, even one stroke, and I will not smite him the second time. But David said to Abisai: Destroy him not, for who can lay his hand on the Lords anointed and be guiltless. And David said furthermore: as sure as the Lord liveth, the Lord shall smite him, or his day shall come to die, or he shall descend into battle and there perish: but the Lord keeps me from laying mine hand upon the Lords anointed. Now then take a fellowship the spear that is at his head, and the cruse of water, and let us go. And David took the spear and the cruse of water that were at Sauls head, and they gat them away, and no man saw or wist it or awoke. For they were all asleep, because the Lord had sent a slumber upon them. Then David went over to the other side and stood on the top of an hill afar off (a great space being between them) and cried to the people and to Abner the son of Ner saying: Answerest thou not Abner? and Abner answered and said: What art thou that criest to the king? and David said to Abner: art not thou a man, and who is like thee in Israel? But wherefore hast thou not kept thy Lord the king? For there came one of the folk to destroy the king thy Lord. It is not good that thou hast done. As truly as the Lord liveth ye are worthy to die, because ye have no better kept the Lords anointed. And now see where the kings spear is and the cruse of water that were at his head.

Then Saul knew Davids voice and said: is this thy voice my son David? and David said: it is my voice my Lord king. And he said thereto wherefore doth my Lord persecute his servant? for what have I done? or what evil is in mine hand? Now hear therefore (my Lord king) the words of thy servant. If the Lord have stirred thee up against me, he shall smell the savour of sacrifice. But and if they be the children of men, cursed be they before the Lord. For they have cast me out from abiding in the inheritance of the Lord, saying: hence and go serve other Gods. And yet I hope my blood shall not fall to the earth before the face of the Lord, though the king of Israel be come out to hunt a flea, as men hunt the partridge in the mountains. Then said Saul: I have sinned, come again my son David for I will do thee no more harm, because my soul was precious in thine eyes this day. Behold, I have played the fool and have erred exceeding much. And David answered and said: behold the kings spear, let one of the young men come over and fetch it.[1] The Lord reward every mans righteousness and sayeth: for the Lord delivered thee into my hand this day, but I would not lay mine hand upon ye Lords anointed. And as thy life was much set by this time in mine eyes: so be my life set by in the eyes of the Lord, that he deliver me out of all tribulation. And Saul said to David: Blessed art thou my son David, for thou shalt be a doer and also able

[1] For 'fetch' he writes 'fet', an early form of the word which has survived in dialect. The same form was used in the Great Bible (*John* xx).

to bring to an end. And so David went his way and Saul turned to his place again.

Psalm XXIII

Psalm of David

The Lord is my shepherd I can want nothing.

He feedeth me in a green pasture and leadeth me to a fresh water.

He quickeneth my soul and bringeth me forth in the way of righteousness for his names sake.

Though I should walk now in the valley of the shadow of death yet I fear no evil for thou art with me: thy staff and thy sheephook comfort me.

Thou preparest a table before me against mine enemies: thou anointest my head with oil, and fillest my cup full.

Oh let thy loving kindness and mercy follow me all the days of my life, that I may dwell in ye house of the Lord for ever.

Psalm CXXI

I lift up mine eyes unto the hills from whence cometh my help.

My help cometh even from the Lord which hath made heaven and earth.

He will not suffer thy foot to be moved and he that keepeth thee sleepeth not.

Behold he that keepeth Israel doth neither slumber nor sleep.

The Lord himself is thy keeper, the Lord is thy defence upon thy right hand.

So that the sun shall not burn thee by day, neither the moon by night.

The Lord preserveth thee from all evil, yea it is the Lord that keepeth thy soul.

The Lord preserveth thy going out and thy coming in from this time forth for ever more.

Psalm CXXII

I was glad, when they said unto me: we will go in to the house of the Lord.

Our feet shall stand in thy gates. O Jerusalem.

Jerusalem is builded as a city, that is at unity in itself.

For there the tribes go up, even the tribes of the Lord: to testify unto Israel, to give thanks unto the name of the Lord.

For there is the seat of judgement, even the seat of the house of David.

O Pray for the peace of Jerusalem, they shall prosper that love thee.

Peace be within thy walls, and plenteousness within thy palaces.

For my brethren and companions sakes, I will wish thee prosperity.

Yea because of the house of the Lord our God, I will seek to do thee good.

Psalm CXXIII

Unto thee lift I up mine eyes, thou that dwellest in the heavens.

Behold, even as the eyes of servants look unto the hands

of their masters: and as the eyes of a maiden unto the hands of her mistress, even so our eyes wait upon the Lord our God, until he have mercy upon us.

Have mercy upon us, O Lord, have mercy upon us, for we are utterly despised.

Our soul is filled with the scornful reproof of the wealthy, and with the despitefulness of the proud.

Psalm CXXIV

If the Lord had not been of our side (now may Israel say). If the Lord had not been of our side, when men rose up against us.

They had swallowed us up quick, when they were so wrathfully displeased at us.

Yea the waters had drowned us, the stream had gone over our soul.

The deep waters of the proud had gone even unto our soul.

But praised be the Lord, which hath not given us over for a prey unto their teeth.

Our soul is escaped, even as a bird out of the snare of the fowler: the snare is broken and we are delivered.

Our help standeth in the name of the Lord, which hath made heaven and earth.

4

JOHN FISHER

This translation of a psalm by the sainted and martyred Bishop of Rochester must serve to represent the many fragmentary biblical versions executed by scholars under Henry VIII; its date is unknown, but it seems to have been made from Latin for courtly use. It was first printed in a 1545 royal prayer book, now a very rare book.

Psalm C.

Rejoice and sing in the honour of the lord, all ye that live on earth,

worship and serve the lord with gladness, come into his sight and presence with joy and mirth.

Acknowledge you, and confess, that the lord is that god, which hath created and made us, for truly we made not ourself, but we be his people and his flock, which he nourisheth and feedeth continually.

Go ye through his gates to give him thanks for the innumerable benefits, which ye have received of him: and to sing through his courts his worthy acts and deeds: praise him, and highly commend his name.

For the lord is both good and gracious, and his mercy is infinite: he is most constant in keeping of his promises, not to one generation only, but even to all.

78

5

THE GREAT BIBLE (1539)

This is the first of the long series of official English Bible versions. Coverdale was commissioned by the Archbishop to revise Matthew's Bible, substantially the work of Tyndale, and the Archbishop wrote a preface; the Bible appeared in 1539, though I have used a 1541 copy for the texts I have reproduced. The Great Bible was censored and revised by several bishops and printed at first in France and then in England, with a display of magnificent elegance perhaps unique among English books of its date. It was an instrument of royal ecclesiastical policy, it was therefore widely received and its status was authoritative for ten years; it continued in use at least into the 1560s.

Genesis VIII

And God remembered Noah, and every beast, and all the cattle that was with him in the Ark. And God made a wind to pass upon the earth, and the waters ceased. The fountains also of the deep and the windows of heaven were stopped, and the rain from heaven was restrained. And the waters from the earth were returned, going and coming again. And after the end of the hundredth and fiftieth day, the waters were abated.

And in the seventh month: in the seventh day of the

Month, the Ark rested upon the mountains of Armenia. And the waters truly were going and decreasing until the tenth month: for in the tenth month, and in the first day of the same month, were the tops of the mountains seen. And after the end of the fortieth day, it happened that Noah opened the window of the Ark which he had made. And he sent forth a raven, which went out going forth and returning again, until the waters were dried up upon the earth. And again he sent forth a dove from him, that he might see if the waters were abated from the upper face of the ground. And the dove found no rest for the sole of her foot, and she returned unto him again into the Ark: for the waters were in the upper face of the whole earth. And he when he had put forth his hand, took her: and pulled her into him into the Ark.

And he abode yet other seven days, and proceeding further, he sent forth the dove out of the Ark. And the dove came to him in the even tide, and lo, in her mouth was an olive leaf that she had plucked: whereby Noah did know, that the waters were abated upon the earth. And he abode yet another seven days, and sent forth the dove, which proceeded not to return unto him any more.

And it came to pass in the six hundred and one year, in the first month, and in the first day of the month, the waters were dried up from the earth. And Noah removed the covering of the Ark, and looked, and behold, the upper face of the ground was dried up. And in the second month, in the seven and twenty day of the month, was the earth dried.

And God spake unto Noah saying: Go forth of the Ark, thou and thy wife, thy sons, and thy sons wives with thee. And bring forth with thee, every beast that is with thee: of all flesh (both foul and cattle, and every worm that creepeth upon the earth) that they may gender in the earth, and bring forth fruit, and increase upon earth. And so Noah came forth, and his sons, his wife, and his sons wives with him. Every beast also and every worm, every fowl, and whatso ever creepeth upon the earth (after their kinds) went out of the Ark.

And Noah builded an altar unto the Lord, and took of every clean beast, and of every clean fowl, and offered sacrifices in the altar. And the Lord smelled a sweet (or quiet) savour. And the Lord said in his heart: I will not proceed to curse the ground any more for mans sake, for the imagination of mans heart is evil even from his youth. Neither will I add to smite any more every thing living, as I have done, yet therefore shall not sowing time and harvest, cold and heat, summer and winter, day and night cease, all the days of the earth.

Leviticus xix

And the Lord spake unto Moses, saying: speak unto all the multitude of the children of Israel, and say unto them: Ye shall be holy, for I the Lord your God am holy. Ye shall fear every man his father and his mother, and keep my Sabbaths: I am the Lord your God. Ye shall not turn unto idols, nor make you gods of metal. I am the Lord your God. If ye offer a peace offering unto the Lord ye shall offer it that ye may be accepted. It shall be eaten the same day ye offer it, and on the morrow. And if aught remain until the third day, it shall be burnt in the fire. And if it be eaten the third day, it is unclean and not accepted. He that eateth it, shall bear his sin, because he hath defiled the hallowed thing of the Lord, and that soul shall perish from among his people.

When ye reap down the ripe corn of your land, ye shall not reap down ye utmost border of your field, neither shalt thou gather that which is left behind in thy harvest. Thou shalt not pluck in all thy vineyard clean, neither gather in the grapes that are overscaped. But thou shalt leave them for the poor and stranger. I am the Lord your God.

Ye shall not steal, neither lie, neither deal falsely one with another. Ye shall not swear by my name in vain: neither shalt thou defile the name of thy God. I am the Lord. Thou shalt not do thy neighbour wrong, neither rob him violently, neither shall the workmans labour abide with thee until the morning. Thou shalt not curse the deaf, neither put a stumbling block before the blind: but shalt fear thy God. I am the Lord. Ye shall do no unrighteousness in judgement. Thou shalt not favour the poor: nor honour the mighty, but in righteousness shalt thou judge thy neighbour.

Thou shalt not go up and down as a privy accuser among thy people, neither shalt thou stand against the blood of thy neighbour. I am the Lord. Thou shalt not hate thy brother in thine heart, but shalt in any wise rebuke thy neighbour: that thou bear not sin for his sake. Thou shalt not avenge thyself, nor be mindful of wrong against the children of my people: but shalt love thy neighbour even as thy self. I am the Lord.

Ye shall keep mine ordinances. Thou shalt not let cattle gender with a contrary kind, neither sow thy field with mingled seed neither shalt thou put on any garment of linen and woollen. Who so ever lieth and meddleth with a woman that is a bond maid, nevertheless appointed to a husband, but not redeemed, nor freedom given her, she shall be scourged with a leathern whip, and they shall not die, because she was not free. And he shall bring for his trespass unto the Lord: before the door of the tabernacle of witness, a ram for a trespass offering. And the Priest shall make an atonement for him with the ram which is for the trespass before the Lord, concerning his sin which he hath done, and the sin which he hath done, shall be forgiven him.

When ye come to the land, and have planted all manner of trees convenient to be eaten of, ye shall put away the foreskin of every one with the fruit thereof: even three year shall they be uncircumcised unto you, and shall not be eaten of. But in the fourth year all the fruit of them shall be holy, and commendable to the Lord. In the fifth year shall ye eat of the fruit of them, and ye may gather in the increase of them. I am the Lord your God.

Ye shall not eat upon blood, neither shall ye use witchcraft, nor observe times. Ye shall not round the locks of your heads, neither shalt thou mar the tufts of thy beard.

Ye shall not rent your flesh for any souls sake, nor print any marks upon you. I am the Lord. Thou shalt not make thy daughter common, that thou wouldest cause her to be an whore: lest the land also fall to whoredom, and be full of wickedness. Ye shall keep my Sabbaths and fear my sanctuary: I am the Lord. Ye shall not regard them that work with spirits neither seek after soothsayers to be defiled by them: I am the Lord your God.

Thou shalt rise up before the hoarhead, and reverence the face of the old man, and dread thy God. I am the Lord. If a stranger sojourn with thee in your land, ye shall not vex him. But the stranger that dwelleth with you, shall be as one of yourselves, and thou shalt love him as thyself, for ye were strangers in the land of Egypt. I am the Lord your God. Ye shall do no unrighteousness in judgement, meteyerde,[1] in weight or in measure. True balances, true weights, a true Epha and a true hyn shall ye have. I am the Lord your God, which brought you out of the land of Egypt. Therefore shall ye observe all mine ordinances: and all my judgements, and do them. I am the Lord.

[1] 'Meteyerde', 'meteyard' or 'meteward' means a measuring rod. Here it is repeated from Coverdale (1535).

Psalm XXIII

Psalm of David

The Lord is my shepherd: therefore can I lack nothing. He shall feed me in a green pasture, and lead me forth beside the waters of comfort. He shall convert my soul, and bring me forth in the paths of righteousness for his names sake. Yea, though I walk through the valley of the shadow of death: I will fear no evil, for thou art with me: thy rod and thy staff comfort me. Thou shalt prepare a table before me against them that trouble me: thou hast anointed my head with oil, and my cup shall be full. But (thy) loving kindness and mercy shall follow me all the days of my life, and I will dwell in the house of the Lord for ever.

John xx

The first day of the Sabbaths, came Mary Magdalen early (when it was yet dark) unto the sepulchre and saw the stone taken away from the grave. Then she ran, and came to Simon Peter, and to the other disciple whom Jesus loved, and sayeth unto them: They have taken away the Lord out of the grave, and we cannot tell where they have laid him. Peter therefore went forth, and that other disciple, and came unto the sepulchre. They ran both together, and the other disciple did outrun Peter, and came first to the sepulchre. And when he had stooped down, he saw the linen clothes lying yet went he not in. Then came Simon Peter following him, and went into the sepulchre, and saw the linen clothes lie, and the napkin that was about his head, not lying with the linen clothes, but wrapped together in a place by itself. Then went in also that other disciple, which came first to the sepulchre, and he saw, and believed. For as yet they knew not the scripture, that he should rise again from death. Then the disciples went away again unto their own home.

Mary stood without at the sepulchre weeping. So as she wept, she bowed herself into the sepulchre, and seeth two angels clothed in white, sitting the one at the head, and the other at the feet, where they had laid the body of Jesus. They say unto her: Woman, why weepest thou? She sayeth unto them: for they have taken away my Lord, and I wot not where they have laid him. When she had thus said, she turned herself back, and saw Jesus standing, and knew not that it was Jesus. Jesus sayeth unto her: Woman, why weepest thou? Whom seekest thou? She supposing that he had been a gardener, sayeth unto him: Sir, if thou hast born him hence, tell me where thou hast laid him, and I will fetch him. Jesus sayeth unto her: Mary. She turned herself, and said unto him: Rabboni, which is to say: master. Jesus sayeth unto her: Touch me not, for I am not yet ascended to my father. But go to my brethren, and say unto them I ascend unto my father and your father: and to my God, and your God. Mary Magdalen came and told the disciples, that she had seen the Lord, and that he had spoken such things unto her. The same day at night which was the first day of the Sabbaths, when the doors were shut (where the disciples were assembled together for fear of the Jews) came Jesus, and stood in the midst, and sayeth unto them: Peace be unto you. And when he had so said, he shewed unto them his hands, and his side. Then were the disciples glad when they saw the Lord. Then said Jesus to them again: peace be unto you. As my father sent me, even so send I you also. And when he had said those words, he breathed on them, and sayeth unto them: Receive ye the holy ghost. Whosoevers sins ye remit, they are remitted unto them. And whosoevers sins ye retain, they are retained.

But Thomas one of the twelve (which is called Didimus)

was not with them when Jesus came. The other disciples therefore said unto him: We have seen the Lord. But he said unto them except I see in his hands the print of the nails, and put my finger into the print of the nails, and thrust my hand into his side, I will not believe. And after eight days again his disciples were within and Thomas with them. Then came Jesus when the doors were shut, and stood in the midst, and said: Peace be unto you. And after that said he to Thomas: bring thy finger hither, and see my hands, and reach hither thy hand, and thrust it into my side, and be not faithless, but believing. Thomas answered and said unto him: my Lord, and my God. Jesus sayeth unto him: Thomas, because thou hast seen me, thou hast believed, blessed are they that have not seen, and yet have believed. And many other signs truly did Jesus in the presence of his disciples, which are not written in this book. These are written that ye might believe, that Jesus is Christ the son of God, and that (in believing) ye might have life through his name.

6

THE GENEVA BIBLE (1560)

The Geneva Bible was the work of English Protestant
exiles under Queen Mary. It was based on Hebrew and
Greek originals, on wide learning, on an intense passion
and on great talent. The chance of the accession of Queen
Elizabeth provided its opportunity. It was printed in 1560
at Geneva and was the first English quarto Bible and the
first in roman type, though its first English edition, which
followed at once, was an old-fashioned folio. It was many
times revised with changing annotations and was the basis
of Cromwell's Soldiers' Bible in the English Civil War. I
have used the 1969 Wisconsin photographic reprint of the
1560 edition which is based on two or three copies in
American libraries.

1 Samuel XXVI

Again the Ziphims came unto Saul to Gibeah, saying, Doeth
not David hide himself in the hill of Hachilah before
Jeshimon?

Then Saul arose, and went down to the wilderness of
Ziph, having three thousand chosen men of Israel with him,
for to take David in the wilderness of Ziph.

And Saul pitched in the hill of Hachilah, which is before
Jeshimon by the way side. Now David abode in the

wilderness, and he saw that Saul came after him into the wilderness.

(For David had sent out spies, & understood that Saul was come in very deed.)

Then David arose, and came to the place where Saul had pitched, and when David beheld the place where Saul lay, & Abner the son of Ner which was his chief captain, (for Saul lay in the fort, and the people pitched round about him.)

Then spake David, & said to Ahimelech the Hittite, and to Abishai the son of Zeruiah, brother to Joab, saying, Who will go down with me to Saul to the host? Then Abishai said, I will go down with thee.

So David and Abishai came down to the people by night: and behold, Saul lay sleeping within the fort, & his spear did stick in the ground at his head: and Abner and the people lay round about him.

Then said Abishai to David, God hath closed mine enemy into thine hand this day: now therefore, I pray thee, let me smite him once with a spear to the earth, and I will not smite him again.

And David said to Abishai, Destroy him not: for who can lay his hand on the Lord's anointed, and be guiltless?

Moreover David said, As the Lord liveth, either the Lord shall smite him, or his day shall come to die, or he shall descend into battle, and perish.

The Lord keep me from laying mine hand upon the Lord's anointed: but, I pray thee, take now the spear that is at his head, and the pot of water, and let us go hence.

So David took the spear and the pot of water from Saul's head, & they gate them away, and no man saw it, nor marked it, neither did any awake, but they were all asleep: for the Lord had sent a dead sleep upon them.

Then David went into the other side, & stood on the top of a hill a far off, a great space being between them.

And David cried to the people, and to Abner the son of Ner, saying, Hearest thou not Abner? Then Abner answered, and said, Who art thou that cryest to the King?

And David said to Abner, Art not thou a man? and who is like thee in Israel? wherefore then hast thou not kept thy lord the King? for there came one of the folk in to destroy the King thy lord.

This is not well done of thee: as the Lord liveth, ye are worthy to die, because ye have not kept your master the Lord's Anointed: and now see where the King's spear is, and pot of water that stood at his head.

And Saul knew David's voice, & said, Is this thy voice, my son David? And David said, It is my voice, my lord O King.

And he said, Wherefore doeth my lord thus persecute his servant? for what have I done? or what evil is in mine hand?

Now therefore, I beseech thee, let my lord the King hear the words of his servant. If the Lord have stirred thee up against me, let him smell the favour of a sacrifice: but if the children of men have done it, cursed be they before the Lord: for they have cast me out this day from abiding in the inheritance of the Lord, saying, Go, serve other gods.

Now therefore let not my blood fall to the earth before the face of the Lord: for the King of Israel is come out to seek a fly, as one would hunt a partridge in the mountains.

Then said Saul, I have sinned: come again, my son David: for I will do thee no more harm, because my soul was precious in thine eyes this day: behold, I have done foolishly, and have erred exceedingly.

Then David answered, & said, Behold the King's spear, let one of the young men come over and fetch it.

And let the Lord reward every man according to his righteousness & faithfulness: for the Lord had delivered into mine hands this day, but I would not lay mine hand upon the Lord's anointed.

And behold, like as thy life was much set by this day in mine eyes: so let my life be set by in the eyes of the Lord, that he may deliver me out of all tribulation.

Then Saul said to David, Blessed art thou, my son David: for thou shalt do great things, and also prevail. So David went his way, and Saul returned to his place.

Job XXXVI

Elihu also proceeded and said,

Suffer me a little, & I will instruct thee: for I have yet to speak on God's behalf.

I will fetch my knowledge a far off & will attribute righteousness unto my Maker.

For truly my words shall not be false, & he that is perfect in knowledge, speaketh with thee.

Behold, the mighty God casteth away none that is mighty & valiant of courage.

He maintaineth not the wicked, but he giveth judgement to the afflicted.

He withdraweth not his eyes from the righteous, but they are with Kings in the throne, where he placeth them forever: thus they are exalted.

And if they be bound in fetters & tied with the cords of affliction,

Then will he show them their work and their sins, because they have been proud.

He openeth also their ear to discipline, and commandeth them that they return from iniquity.

If they obey and serve him, they shall end their days in prosperity, & their years in pleasures.

But if they will not obey, they shall pass by the sword, & perish without knowledge.

But the hypocrites of heart increase the wrath: for they call not when he bindeth them.

Their soul dyeth in youth, & their life among the whoremongers.

He delivereth the poor in his affliction, and openeth their ear in trouble.

Even so would he have taken thee out of the straight place into a broad place & not shut up beneath [*sic*] and that which resteth upon thy table, had been full of fat.

But thou art full of the judgement of the wicked, though judgement and equity maintain all things.

For God's wrath is, lest he should take thee away in thine abundance: for no multitude of gifts can deliver thee.

Will he regard thy riches? he regardeth not gold, nor all them that excel in strength.

Be not careful in the night, how he destroyeth the people out of their place.

Take thou heed: look not to iniquity: for thou hast chosen it rather than affliction.

Behold, God exalteth by his power: what teacher is like him?

Who hath appointed to him his way? or who can say, Thou hast done wickedly?

Remember that thou magnify his work, which men behold.

All men see it, and men behold it a far off.

Behold, God is excellent, & we know him not, neither can the number of his years be searched out.

When he restraineth the drops of water, the rain poureth down by the vapour thereof,

Which rain the clouds do drop & let fall abundantly upon man.

Who can know the divisions of the clouds? & the thunders of his tabernacle?

Behold he spreadeth his light upon it, and covereth the bottom of the sea.

For thereby he judgeth the people, and giveth meat abundantly.

He covereth the light with the clouds, and commandeth them to go against it.

His companion showeth him thereof, and there is anger in rising up.

Job XL. 10–26

Behold now Behemoth (whom I made with thee) which eateth grass as an ox.

Behold now, his strength is in his loins, and his force is in the navel of his belly.

When he taketh pleasure, his tail is like a cedar: the sinews of his stones are wrapt together.

His bones are like staves of brass, and his small bones like staves of iron.

He is the chief of the ways of God: he that made him, will make his sword to approach unto him.

Surely the mountains bring him forth grass, where all the beasts of the field play.

Lyeth he under the trees in the covert of the reed and fens?

Can the trees cover him with their shadow? or can the willows of the river compass him about?

Behold, he spoileth the river, and hasteth not: he trusteth that he can draw up Jorden into his mouth.

He taketh it with his eyes, and thrusteth his nose through whatsoever meeteth him.

Canst thou draw out Leviathan with an hook, and with a line which thou shalt cast down unto his tongue?

Canst thou cast a hook into his nose? canst thou pierce his jaws with an angle?

Will he make many prayers unto thee, or speak thee fair?

Will he make a covenant with thee? and wilt thou take him as a servant forever?

Wilt thou play with him as with a bird? or wilt thou bind him for thy maids?

Shall the companions (banquet) with him? shall they divide him among the merchants?

Canst thou fill the basket with his skin? or the fishpannier with his head?

Psalm v

Hear my words, O Lord: understand my meditation.

Hearken unto the voice of my cry, my King & my God: for unto thee do I pray.

Hear my voice in the morning, O Lord: for in the morning will I direct me unto thee, and I will wait.

For thou art not a God that loveth wickedness: neither shall evil dwell with thee.

The foolish shall not stand in thy sight: for thou hatest all them that work iniquity.

Thou shalt destroy them that speak lies: the Lord will abhor the bloody man and deceitful.

But I will come unto thine house in the multitude of thy mercy: & in thy fear will I worship toward thine holy Temple.

Lead me, O Lord, in thy righteousness, because of mine enemies: make thy way plain before my face.

For no constancy is in their mouth: within, they are very corruption: their throat is an open sepulchre, & they flatter with their tongue.

Destroy them, O God: let them fall from their counsel: cast them out for the multitude of their iniquities, because they have rebelled against thee.

And let all them that trust in thee, rejoice & triumph forever, & cover thou them: and let them, that love thy Name, rejoice in thee.

For thou Lord wilt bless the righteous, & with favour wilt compass him, as with a shield.

Psalm LXXXVIII

O Lord God of my salvation, I cry day and night before thee.

Let my prayer enter into thy presence: incline thine ear unto my cry.

For my soul is filled with evils, and my life draweth near to the grave.

I am counted among them that go down unto the pit, and am as a man without strength:

Free among the dead, like the slain lying in the grave, whom thou rememberest no more, and they are cut off from thine hand.

Thou hast layed me in the lowest pit, in darkness, & in the deep.

Thine indignation lieth upon me, and thou hast vexed me with all thy waves. Selah.

Thou hast put away my acquaintance far from me, & made me to be abhorred of them: I am shut up, and cannot get forth.

Mine eye is sorrowful through mine affliction: Lord, I call daily upon thee: I stretch out mine hands unto thee.

Wilt thou show a miracle to the dead? or shall the dead rise & praise thee? Selah.

Shall thy loving kindness be declared in the grave? or thy faithfulness in destruction?

Shall thy wondrous works be known in the dark? and thy righteousness in the land of oblivion?

But unto thee have I cried, O Lord, and early shall my prayer come before thee.

Lord, why dost thou reject my soul, & hidest thy face from me?

I am afflicted and at the point of death: from my youth I suffer thy terrors, doubting of my life.

Isaiah XXIII. 1–11

The burden of Tyrus. Howl, ye ships of Tarshish: for it is destroyed, so that there is none house: none shall come from the land of Chittim: it is revealed unto them.

Be still, ye that dwell in the isles: the merchants of Zidon, & such as pass over the sea, have replenished thee.

The seed of Nilus growing by the abundance of waters, and the harvest of the river was her revenues, and she was a mart of the nations.

Be ashamed, thou Zidon: for the sea hath spoken, even the strength of the sea, saying, I have not travailed, nor brought forth children, neither nourished young men nor brought up virgins.

When the fame cometh to the Egyptians, they shall be sorry, concerning the rumour of Tyrus.

Go you over to Tarshish: howl, ye that dwell in the isles.

Is not this that your glorious city? her antiquity is of ancient days: her own feet shall lead her a far off to be a foreigner.

Who hath decreed this against Tyrus (that crowneth men) whose merchants are princes? whose chapmen are the nobles of the world?

The Lord of hosts hath decreed this, to stain the pride of all glory, and to bring to contempt all them that be glorious in the earth.

Pass through thy land like a flood to the daughter of Tarshish: there is no more strength.

He stretched out his hand upon the sea: he shook the kingdoms: the Lord hath given a commandment concerning the place of merchandise, to destroy the power thereof.

Psalm CVIII

O God, mine heart is prepared, so is my tongue: I will sing & give praise.

Awake viol & harp: I will awake early.

I will praise thee, O Lord, among the people, and I will sing unto thee among the nations.

For thy mercy is great above the heavens, and thy truth unto the clouds.

Exalt thyself, O God, above the heavens, and let thy glory be upon all the earth,

That thy beloved may be delivered: help with thy right hand and hear me.

God has spoken in his holiness: therefore I will rejoice. I shall divide Shechem and measure the valley of Succoth.

Gilead shall be mine, and Manasseh shall be mine: Ephraim also shall be the strength of mine head: Juda is my Lawgiver.

Moab shall be my washpot: over Edom will I cast out my shoe: upon Palestina will I triumph.

Who will lead me into the strong city? who will bring me unto Edom?

Wilt not thou, O God, which haddest forsaken us, & didst not go forth, O God, with our armies?

Give us help against trouble: for vain is the help of man.

Through God we shall do valiantly: for he shall tread down our enemies.

Psalm LXXXVIII. 16–18

Thine indignations go over me, & thy fear hath cut me off.

They came round about me daily like water, & compassed me together.

My lovers and friends hast thou put away from me, and mine acquaintance hid themselves.

Psalm XXIII

The Lord is my shepherd, I shall not want.

He maketh me to rest in green pastures, & leadeth me by the still waters.

He restoreth my soul, & leadeth me in the paths of righteousness for his Name's sake.

Yea, though I should walk through the valley of the shadow of death, I will fear no evil: for thou art with me: thy rod and thy staff, they comfort me.

Thou dost prepare a table before me, in the sight of mine adversaries: thou dost anoint mine head with oil, and my cup runneth over.

Doubtless kindness, & mercy shall follow me all the days of my life, and I shall remain a long season in the house of the Lord.

Matthew XXVII. 17–53

When they were then gathered together, Pilate said unto them, Whether will ye that I let loose unto you Barabbas, or Jesus which is called Christ?

(For he knew well, that for envy they had delivered him.

D

Also when he was set down upon the judgement seat, his wife sent to him, saying, Have thou nothing to do with that just man: for I have suffered many things this day in a dream by reason of him.)

But the chief Priests & the Elders had persuaded the people that they should ask Barabbas, and should destroy Jesus.

Then the governor answered, and said unto them, Whether of the twain will ye that I let loose unto you? And they said, Barabbas.

Pilate said unto them, What shall I do then with Jesus which is called Christ? They all said to him, Let him be crucified.

Then said the governor, But what evil hath he done? Then they cried the more, saying, Let him be crucified.

When Pilate saw that he availed nothing, but that more tumult was made, he took water and washed his hands before the multitude, saying, I am innocent of the blood of this just man: look you to it.

Then answered all the people, and said, His blood be on us, and on our children.

Thus let he Barabbas loose unto them, and scourged Jesus, and delivered him to be crucified.

Then the soldiers of the governor took Jesus into the common hall, and gathered about him the whole band.

And they stripped him, & put upon him a scarlet robe,

And plaited a crown of thorns, and put it upon his head, and a reed in his right hand, and bowed their knees before him, and mocked him, saying, God save thee King of the Jews,

And spitted upon him, and took a reed, and smote him on the head.

Thus when they had mocked him, they took the robe from him, and put his own raiment on him, and led him away to crucify him.

Matthew XXVII

And as they came out, they found a man of Cyrene, named Simon: him they compelled to bear his cross.

And when they came unto the place called Golgotha, (that is to say, the place of dead men's skulls)

They gave him vinegar to drink, mingled with gall: and when he had tasted thereof, he would not drink.

And when they had crucified him, they parted his garments, & did cast lots, that it might be fulfilled, which was spoken by the Prophet, They divided my garments among them, and upon my vesture did cast lots.

And they sat, and watched him there.

They set up also over his head his cause written, THIS IS JESUS. THE KING OF THE JEWS.

And there were two thieves crucified with him, one on the right hand, and another on the left.

And they that passed by, reviled him, wagging their heads,

And saying, Thou that destroyest the Temple, and buildest it in three days, save thyself: if thou be the Son of God, come down from the cross.

Likewise also the high Priests mocking him, with the Scribes, and Elders, and Pharisees, said,

He saved others, but he cannot save himself: if he be the King of Israel, let him now come down from the cross, and we will believe him.

He trusteth in God, let him deliver him now, if he will have him: for he said, I am the Son of God.

That same also the thieves which were crucified with him, cast in his teeth.

Now from the sixth hour was there darkness over all the land, unto the ninth hour.

And about the ninth hour Jesus cried with a loud voice,

saying, Eli, Eli, lama sabacthani? that is, My God, why hast thou forsaken me?

And some of them that stood there, when they heard it, said, This man calleth Elias.

And straight way one of them ran, and took a sponge, and filled it with vinegar, and put it on a reed, and gave him to drink.

Others said, Let be: let us see if Elias will come and save him.

Then Jesus cried again with a loud voice, and yielded up the ghost.

And behold, the veil of the Temple was rent in twain, from the top to the bottom, and the earth did quake, and the stones were cloven,

And the graves did open themselves, & many bodies of the Saints which slept, arose,

And came out of the graves after his resurrection, and went into the holy City, and appeared unto many.

John 1. 1–14

In the beginning was the Word, and the Word was with God and that Word was God.

The same was in the beginning with God.

All things were made by it, & without it was made nothing that was made.

In it was life, and the life was the light of men.

And the light shineth in the darkness, & the darkness comprehended it not.

There was a man sent from God, whose name was John.

The same came for a witness, to bear witness of the light that all men through him might believe.

He was not that light, but was sent to bear witness of the light.

That was the true light, which lighteth every man that cometh into the world.

He was in the world, and the world was made by him: & the world knew him not.

He came unto his own, and his own received him not.

But as many as received him, to them he gave power to be the sons of God, even to them that believe in his Name,

Which are born not of blood, nor of the will of the flesh, nor of the will of man, but of God.

And the Word was made flesh, and dwelt among us, (and we saw the glory thereof, as the glory of the only begotten Son of the Father) full of grace and truth.

Romans v

Then being justified by faith, we have peace toward God through our Lord Jesus Christ.

By whom also we have access through faith unto this grace, wherein we stand, & rejoice under the hope of the glory of God.

Neither do we so only, but also we rejoice in tribulations, knowing that tribulation bringeth forth patience, and patience experience, and experience hope,

And hope maketh not ashamed, because the love of God is shed abroad in our hearts by the holy Ghost, which is given unto us.

For Christ, when we were yet of no strength, at his time, died for the ungodly.

Doubtless one will scarce die for a righteous man: but yet for a good man it may be that one dare die.

But God setteth out his love towards us, being the while we were yet sinners, Christ died for us.

Much more then, being now justified by his blood, we shall be saved from wrath through him.

For if when we were enemies, we were reconciled to God by the death of his Son, much more being reconciled, we shall be saved by his life.

And not only so, but we also rejoice in God through our Lord Jesus Christ, by whom we have now received the atonement.

Wherefore, as by one man sin entered into the world, and death by sin, and so death went over all men: for as much as all men have sinned.

For unto the time of the Law was sin in the world, but sin is not imputed, while there is no Law.

But death reigned from Adam to Moses even over them also that sinned not after the manner of the transgression of Adam, which was the figure of him that was to come.

But yet the gift is not so, as is the offence: for if through the offence of one, many be dead, much more the grace of God, and the gift by grace, which is by one man Jesus Christ, hath abounded unto many.

Neither is the gift so, as that which entered in by one that sinned: for the fault came of one offence unto condemnation: but the gift is of many offences to justification.

For if by the offence of one, death reigned through one, much more shall they which receive the abundance of grace, and of the gift of righteousness, reign in life through one, that is Jesus Christ.

Likewise then as by the offence of one the fault came on all men to condemnation, so by the justifying of one the benefit abounded toward all men to the justification of life.

For as by one man's disobedience many were made sinners, so by the obedience of one shall many also be made righteous.

Moreover the Law entered thereupon that the offence

should abound: nevertheless where sin abounded, there grace abounded much more:

That as sin had reigned unto death, so might grace also reign by righteousness unto eternal life, through Jesus Christ our Lord.

Romans VI

What shall we say then? Shall we continue still in sin, that grace may abound? God forbid.

How shall we, that are dead to sin, live yet therein?

Know ye not, that all we which have been baptized into Jesus Christ, have been baptized into his death?

We are buried then with him by baptism into his death, that like as Christ was raised up from the dead by the glory of the Father, so we also should walk in newness of life.

For if we be grafted with him to the similitude of his death, even so shall we be to the similitude of his resurrection,

Knowing this, that our old man is crucified with him, that the body of sin might be destroyed, that henceforth we should not serve sin.

For he that is dead, is freed from sin.

Wherefore, if we be dead with Christ, we believe that we shall live also with him,

Knowing that Christ being raised from the dead, dyeth no more: death hath no more dominion over him.

For in that he died, he died once to sin: but in that he liveth, he liveth to God.

Likewise think ye also, that ye are dead to sin, but are alive to God in Jesus Christ our Lord.

Let not sin reign therefore in your mortal body, that ye should obey it in the lusts thereof.

Neither give ye your members as weapons of unrighteousness unto sin: but give yourselves unto God, as they that are alive from the dead, and give your members as weapons of righteousness unto God.

For sin shall not have domination over you: for ye are not under the Law, but under grace.

What then? shall we sin because we are not under the Law, but under grace? God forbid.

Know ye not, that to whomsoever ye give yourselves as servants to obey, his servants ye are to whom ye obey, whether it be of sin unto death, or of obedience unto righteousness?

But God be thanked, that ye have been the servants of sin, but ye have obeyed from the heart unto the form of the doctrine, whereunto ye were delivered.

Being then made free from sin, ye are made the servants of righteousness.

I speak after the manner of man, because of the infirmity of your flesh: for as ye have given your members servants to uncleanness and to iniquity, to commit iniquity, so now give your members servants unto righteousness in holiness.

For when ye were the servants of sin, ye were freed from righteousness.

What fruit had ye then in those things, whereof ye are not ashamed? For the end of those things is death.

But now being freed from sin, and made servants unto God, ye have your fruit in holiness, and the end, everlasting life.

For the wages of sin is death: but the gift of God is eternal life through Jesus Christ our Lord.

Revelation XVIII

And after these things, I saw another Angel come down from heaven, having great power, so that the earth was lightened with his glory.

And he cried out mightily with a loud voice, saying, It is fallen, it is fallen, Babylon the great city, & is become the habitation of devils, and the hold of all foul spirits, and a cage of every unclean and hateful bird.

For all nations have drunk of the wine of the wrath of her fornication, and the Kings of the earth have committed fornication with her, and the merchants of the earth are waxed rich of the abundance of her pleasures.

And I heard another voice from heaven say, Go out of her, my people, that ye be not partakers in her sins, and that ye receive not of her plagues.

For her sins are come up unto heaven, and God hath remembered her iniquities.

Reward her, even as she hath rewarded you, and give her double according to her works: & in the cup that she hath filled to you, fill her the double.

Inasmuch as she glorified herself, and lived in pleasure, so much give ye to her torment and sorrow: for she saith in her heart, I sit being a queen and am no widow, and shall see no mourning.

Therefore shall her plagues come at one day, death, and sorrow, and famine, & she shall be burnt with fire: for strong is the Lord God which will condemn her.

And the Kings of the earth shall bewail her, & lament for her, which have committed fornication, & lived in pleasure with her, when they shall see the smoke of her burning,

And shall stand a far off for fear of her torment, saying, Alas, alas, the great city Babylon, the mighty city: for in one hour is thy judgement come.

And the merchants of the earth shall weep and wail over her: for no man buyeth their ware any more.

The ware of gold and silver, and of precious stone, and of pearls, and of fine linen, and of purple, and of silk, and of scarlet, & of all manner of Thyne wood, and of all vessels of ivory, and of all vessels of most precious wood, & of brass, and of iron, and of marble,

And of cinnamon, and odours, and ointments, and frankincense, and wine, and oil, and fine flour, and wheat, & beasts and sheep, and horses, and chariots,[1] & servants, and souls of men.

(And the apples that thy soul lusted after, are departed from thee, & all things which were fat and excellent, are departed from thee, and thou shalt find them no more)

The merchants of these things which were waxed rich, shall stand a far off from her, for fear of her torment, weeping and wailing,

And saying, Alas, alas, the great city, that was clothed in fine linen and purple, and scarlet, and gilded with gold, and precious stone, and pearls.

For in one hour so great riches are come to desolation. And every ship master, and all the people that occupy ships, and shipmen, and whosoever travail on the sea,[2] shall stand a far off,

And cry, when they see the smoke of her burning, saying, What city was like unto this great city?

And they shall cast dust on their heads, and cry weeping, and wailing, & say, Alas, alas, the great city, wherein were made rich all that had ships on the sea by her costliness: for in one hour she is made desolate.

---

[1] In the text 'chariots' is given in the form 'charrets'.

[2] In the phrase 'whosoever travail on the sea' 'travail' and not 'travel' is certainly meant; it translates *'ergazontai'* (*'operantur'*).

O heaven, rejoice of her, and ye holy Apostles and Prophets: for God hath given your judgement on her.

Then a mighty Angel took up a stone like a great millstone, & cast it into the sea, saying. With such violence shall the great city Babylon be cast, and shall be found no more.

And the voices of harpers, & musicians, and of pipers, & trumpeters shall be heard no more in thee, and no craftsman, of whatsoever craft he be, shall be found any more in thee: and the sound of a millstone shall be heard no more in thee.

And the light of a candle shall shine no more in thee: and the voice of the bridegroom and of the bride shall be heard no more in thee: for thy merchants were the great men of the earth: and with thine enchantments were deceived all nations.

And in her was found the blood of the Prophets, and of the Saints, and of all that were slain upon the earth.

Revelation XIX

And after these things I heard a great voice of a great multitude in heaven, saying, Hallelu-iah, salvation & glory, and honour, and power be to the Lord our God.

For true and righteous are his judgements: for he hath condemned the great whore, which did corrupt the earth with her fornication, and hath avenged the blood of his servants shed by her hand.

And again they said, Hallelu-iah: & her smoke rose up for evermore.

And the four and twenty Elders, & the four beasts fell down, and worshipped God that sat on the throne, saying, Amen, Hallelu-iah.

Then a voice came out of the throne, saying, Praise our

God, all ye his servants, and ye that fear him, both small and great.

And I heard like a voice of a great multitude, and as the voice of many waters, and as the voice of strong thunderings, saying, Hallelu-iah: for our Lord God almighty hath reigned.

Let us be glad and rejoice, and give glory to him: for the marriage of the Lamb is come, and his wife hath made herself ready.

And to her was granted, that she should be arrayed with pure fine linen and shining, for the fine linen is the righteousness of Saints.

Then he said unto me, Write, Blessed are they which are called unto the Lamb's supper. And he said unto me, These words of God are true.

And I fell before his feet to worship him: but he said unto me, See thou do it not: I am thy fellow servant, and one of thy brethren, which have the testimony of Jesus. Worship God: for the testimony of Jesus, is the spirit of prophecy.

And I saw heaven open, and behold a white horse, and he that sat upon him, was called, Faithful & true, & he judgeth and fighteth righteously.

And his eyes were as a flame of fire, & on his head were many crowns: and he had a name written, that no man knew but himself.

And he was clothed with a garment dipped in blood, and his name is called, THE WORD OF GOD.

And the warriors which were in heaven, followed him upon white horses, clothed with fine linen white and pure.

And out of his mouth went out a sharp sword, that with it he should smite the heathen: for he shall rule them with a rod of iron: for he it is that treadeth the wine press of the fierceness and wrath of almighty God.

The Geneva Bible (1560)

And he hath upon his garment, and upon his thigh a name written, THE KING OF KINGS, AND LORD OF LORDS.

And I saw an Angel stand in the sun, who cried with a loud voice, saying to all the fowls that did fly by the midst of heaven, Come, and gather yourselves together unto the supper of the great God.

That ye may eat the flesh of Kings, & the flesh of his Captains, and the flesh of mighty men, and the flesh of horses, and of them that sit on them, and the flesh of all free men and bondsmen, and of small and great.

And I saw the beast, and the Kings of the earth, and their warriors gathered together to make battle against him, that sat on the horse & against his soldiers.

But the beast was taken, and with him that false prophet that wrought miracles before him, whereby he deceived them that received the beasts mark, & them that worshipped his image. These both were alive cast into a lake of fire, burning with brimstone.

And the remnant were slain with the sword of him that sitteth upon the horse, which cometh out of his mouth, and all the fowls were filled with their flesh.

7

THE BISHOPS' BIBLE (1568)

Between 1561 and 1568 Archbishop Parker and his colleagues revised the old Great Bible of Henry VIII; the result was a blackletter folio of some splendour but few other attractions. The work done was essentially intended as scholarship; Latin translations of the Hebrew text were used in an attempt to improve Coverdale's version. The Bishop's Bible was brought into obligatory use by a decree of Convocation of 1571, and was in fact widely used, at least in the eighties. It was still the official English Bible at the accession of James I, and it was issued in its most recent printing to the scholars who worked on the Authorized Version, for which it was even then still thought to be the proper foundation.

Leviticus XXIV

And the Lord spake unto Moses, saying:

Command the children of Israel that they bring unto thee pure oil olive beaten for the light, to cause the lamps to burn continually,

Without the veil of witness in the tabernacle of the congregation shall Aaron dress them both evening and morning before the Lord always: Let it be a law for ever in your generations.

He shall dress the lamps upon the pure candlestick before the Lord perpetually.

And thou shalt take fine flour, and bake twelve cakes thereof, two tenth deals[1] shall be in one cake.

And thou shalt set them in two rows, six on a row, upon the pure table before the Lord.

And put pure frankincense upon the rows, that they may be bread of remembrance, and an offering made by fire unto the Lord.

Every Sabbath he shall put them in rows before the Lord evermore, of the children of Israel shall they be offered for an everlasting covenant.

And they shall be Aarons and his sons, which shall eat them in the holy place: For they are most holy unto him of the offerings of the Lord made by fire, by a perpetual statute.

And the son of an Israelitish wife, whose father was an Egyptian, went out among the children of Israel: And this son of the Israelitish wife and a man of Israel strove together in the host.

And the Israelitish woman's son blasphemed the name of the Lord, and cursed, and they brought him unto Moses: his mothers name was Selomith, which was the daughter of Dibri, of the tribe of Dan.

And they put him in ward, that the mind of the Lord might be shewed them.

And the Lord spake unto Moses, saying:

Bring the cursed speaker without the host, and let all that heard him, put their hands upon his head, and let all the multitude stone him.

And thou shalt speak unto the children of Israel, saying: whosoever curseth his God, shall bear his sin.

[1] A 'deal' is a part or measure; Coverdale uses the same word in *Leviticus* in 1535.

And he that blasphemeth the name of the Lord, let him be slain, and all the multitude shall stone him to death: whether he be born in the land, or a stranger, when he blasphemeth the name of the Lord, let him be slain.

And he that killeth any man, let him die the death.

And he that killeth a beast, let him make him good, beast for beast.

And if a man cause a blemish in his neighbour: as he hath done, so shall it be done to him.

Broke for broke,[1] eye for eye, and tooth for tooth: even as he hath blemished a man, so shall he be blemished again.

And he that killeth a beast, let him restore it: and he that killeth a man, let him die.

Ye shall have one manner of law, even for the stranger as well as for one of your own country: for I am the Lord your God.

And Moses told the children of Israel, and they brought him that had cursed out of the host, and stoned him with stones: And the children of Israel did as the Lord commanded Moses.

Leviticus xxv. 1–46

And the Lord spake unto Moses in Mount Sinai, saying:

Speak unto the children of Israel, and say unto them: when ye be came into the land which I give you, the land shall rest and keep Sabbath unto the Lord.

Six years thou shalt sow thy field, and six years thou shalt cut thy vineyard, and gather in the fruit thereof.

But the seventh year shall be a Sabbath of rest unto the

---

[1] 'Broke for broke' means 'tit for tat'; the word is cognate to 'broker' and implies repayment for goods received, but it does not seem to be recorded as a noun.

land, the Lords Sabbath it shall be: thou shalt neither sow thy field, nor cut thy vineyard.

That which groweth of the own accord of thy harvest, thou shalt not reap, neither gather the grapes that thou hast left behind: for it is a year of rest unto the land.

And the rest of the land shall be meat for you, even for thee, for thy servant, and for thy maid, for thy hired servant, and for the stranger that sojourneth with thee:

And for thy cattle, and for the beasts that are in thy land, shall all the increase thereof be meat.

And thou shalt number seven Sabbaths of years unto thee, even seven times seven year, and the space of the seven Sabbaths of years will be unto thee nine and forty years.

And then thou shalt cause to blow the trumpet of the Jubilee in the tenth day of the seventh month, even in the day of atonement shall ye make the trumpet blow throughout all your land.

And ye shall hallow that year, even the fiftieth year, and proclaim liberty throughout all the land unto all the inhabiters thereof: for it shall be a Jubilee unto you, and ye shall return every man unto his possession, and every man unto his kindred again.

A year of Jubilee shall that fiftieth year be unto you: Ye shall not sow, neither reap that which growth of it self, neither gather the grapes that are left:

For that year of Jubilee shall be holy unto you: but ye shall eat of the increase thereof out of the field.

In the year of this Jubilee ye shall return every man unto his possession again.

If thou sellest aught unto thy neighbour, or buyest aught of thy neighbour's hand, ye shall not oppress one another.

But according to the number of years after the Jubilee year thou shalt buy of thy neighbour: and according unto the number of years of the fruits he shall sell unto thee.

According unto the multitude of years he shall increase the price thereof, and according to the fewness of years, he shall minish the price of it: for the number of fruits doth he sell unto thee.

Oppress not ye therefore every man his neighbour, but thou shalt fear thy God: For I am the Lord your God.

Wherefore ye shall do after mine ordinances, and keep my laws, and do them, and ye shall dwell in the land in safety.

And the land shall give her fruit, and ye shall eat your fill, and dwell therein in safety.

And if ye shall say, what shall we eat the seventh year? for we shall not sow, nor gather in our increase:

I will send my blessing upon you in the sixth year, and it shall bring forth fruit for three years.

And ye shall sow the eighth year, and eat yet of old fruit until the ninth year: even until her fruits come ye shall eat of old store.

The land shall not be sold to waste: for the land is mine, and ye be but strangers and sojourners with me.

In all the land of your possession, ye shall grant a redemption for the land.

If thy brother be waxed poor, and hath sold away of his possession, and if any of his kin come to redeem it, let him buy out that which his brother sold.

And if he have no man to redeem it, and his hand hath gotten and found as much as may be sufficient to buy it out again:

Then let him count how long it hath been sold, and deliver the rest unto the man to whom he sold it, that he may return to his possession again.

But and if his hand cannot get sufficient to restore to the other again, then that which is sold that remain in the hand of him that hath bought it, until the year of Jubilee: and in the Jubilee it shall come out, and he shall return unto his possession again.

And if a man sell a dwelling house in a walled city, he may buy it out again within a whole year after it is sold: within a year may he redeem it.

But and if he buy it not out again within the space of a full year, then the house that is in the walled city, shall be stablished, as translated to him that bought it and his successors after him, and shall not go out in the Jubilee.

But the houses of villages, which have no walls round about them, are counted as the field of the country: and therefore they may be bought out again, and shall go out in the Jubilee.

Notwithstanding, the cities of the Levites, and the houses of the cities of their possession, may the Levites redeem at all seasons.

And if a man purchase of the Levites, the house that was sold, and the city of their possession, shall go out in the year of Jubilee: for the houses of the cities of the Levites, are their possession among the children of Israel.

But the field of the suburbs of their cities may not be sold: for it is their perpetual possession.

If thy brother be waxen poor and fallen in decay with thee, thou shalt relieve him as a stranger or sojourner, that he may live with thee.

And thou shalt take none usury of him, or vantage: but thou shalt fear thy God, that thy brother may live with thee.

Thou shalt not give him thy money upon usury, nor lend him thy victuals for increase.

I am the Lord your God, which brought you out of the land of Egypt, to give you the land of Chanaan, and to be your God.

If thy brother that dwelleth by thee be waxen poor, and be sold unto thee, thou shalt not compel him to serve as a bond servant:

But as an hired servant, and as a sojourner he shall be with thee, and shall serve thee unto the year of Jubilee.

And then shall he depart from thee, both he and his children with him, and shall return unto his own kindred again, and unto the possession of his fathers shall he return.

For they are my servants, which I brought out of the land of Egypt, and shall not therefore be sold as bondsmen.

Thou shalt not rule over him cruelly, but shalt fear thy God.

Thy bondservant and thy bondmaid which thou shalt have, shall be of the heathen that are round about you: of them shall ye purchase servants and maids.

Moreover, of the children of the strangers that are sojourners among you, of them shall ye buy, and of their families that are with you, which they begat in your land: these shall be your possession.

Judges XVI. 4–31

And after this, he loved a woman by the river of Sorek, whose name was Dalila.

Unto whom came the lords of the Philistines, and said unto her: Persuade him, and see wherein his great strength lyeth, and by what means we may overcome him, that we may bind him and punish him: and every one of us shall give thee eleven hundred silver lynges.[1]

And Dalila said to Samson: Oh, tell me where thy great strength lyeth, and how thou mightest be bound and brought under.

Samson answered unto her: If they bind me with seven green withies that were never dried, I shall be weak, and be as another man.

[1] 'Eleven hundred silver lynges' defeats me, unless (surely not) it should be some corruption of shillings. The word 'lynge' is an obsolete form of 'line'.

And the lords of the Philistines brought her seven withies that were yet green and never dried, and she bound him therewith.

(Notwithstanding she had men lying in wait with her in the chamber): And she said unto him, the Philistines be upon thee Samson. And immediately he brake the cords, as a string of tow breaketh when it feeleth fire. And so his strength was not known.

And Dalila said unto Samson: See, thou hast mocked me, and told me lies: Now therefore tell me wherewith thou mightest be bound.

He answered her: If they bind me with new ropes that never were occupied, I shall be weak, and be as another man.

Dalila therefore took new ropes, and bound him therewith, and said unto him, The Philistines be upon thee Samson. (And there were lyers of wait in the chamber.) And he brake them from of his arms, as they had been but a thread.

And Dalila said unto Samson, hitherto thou hast beguiled me, and told me lies: Yet tell me how thou mightest be bound. He said unto her: If thou plaitest the seven locks of my head the threads of the woof.

And she fastened it with a pin, and said unto him: The Philistines be upon thee Samson. And he awaked out of his sleep, and went away with the pin of the web and the woof.

And she said unto him again: How canst thou say I love thee, when thine heart is not with me? Thou hast mocked me this three times, and hast not told me wherein thy great strength lyeth.

And as she lay upon him with her words, continually vexing of him, his soul was encumbered even unto the death.

And so he told her all his heart, and said unto her: There never came razor upon mine head, for I have been a

Nazarite unto God, even from my mothers womb: Therefore when I am shaven, my strength will go from me, and I shall wax weak, and be like all [other] men.

And when Dalila saw that he had told her all his heart, she sent and called for the lords of the Philistines, saying: Come up yet this once, for he hath shewed me all his heart. Then the Lords of the Philistines come up unto her, and brought the money in their hands.

And she made him sleep upon her knees, and she sent for a man, and he did shave off the seven locks of his head, and began to vex him, and his strength was gone from him.

And she said, the Philistines be upon thee Samson. And he awoke out of his sleep, and said: I will go out now as at other times before, and shake myself. And he wist not that the Lord was departed from him.

But the Philistines took him, and put out his eyes, and brought him down to Azzah, and bound him with fetters of brass: and he did grind in the prison house.

Nowbeit the hair of his head began to grow again after that he was shaven.

Then the lords of the Philistines gathered them together, for to offer a solemn offering unto Dagon their God, and to rejoice: For they said, Our God hath delivered Samson our enemy into our hands.

And when the people saw him, they praised their God: for they said, Our God hath delivered into our hands our enemy, and destroyer of our country, which slew many of us.

And when their hearts were merry, they said: Send for Samson, that he may make us laugh. And they fetched Samson out of the prison house, and he played before them: and they set him between the pillars.

And Samson said unto the lad that led him by the hand: Set me that I may touch the pillars that the house standeth upon. and that I may lean to them.

And the house was full of men and women, and there were all the lords of the Philistines: And there were upon the roof a three thousand men and women that beheld while Samson played.

And Samson called upon the Lord, and said: O Lord God I pray thee think upon me, and strengthen me I beseech thee at this time onelie O God, that I may be at once avenged of the Philistines for my two eyes.

And Samson caught the two middle pillars on which the house stood and on which it was borne up, the one in his right hand, and the other in his left.

And Samson said: My soul shall die with the Philistines, and bowed them with all his might, and the house fell upon the lords and upon all the people that were therein: And so the dead which he slew at his death, were more than they which he slew in his life.

And then his brethren and all the house of his father came down, and took him up, and brought him, and buried him between Zarah and Esthaol, in the burying place of Manoah his father: And he judged Israel twenty years.

1 Samuel VI

And the ark of the Lord was in the country of the Philistines seven months.

And the Philistines called for the priests and the soothsayers, saying: What shall we do with the ark of the Lord? Tell us wherewith we shall send it home again:

They said: If you send away the ark of the God of Israel, send it not empty: but reward it with sin offering, and then ye shall be whole, and it shall be known to you why his hand departeth not from you.

Then said they: And what shall be the sin offering, which

we shall reward him with? They answered: five golden emerodes,[1] and five golden mice, according to the number of the princes of the Philistines: For one plague was on you all, and on your princes.

Wherefore ye shall make images like to your emerodes, and images like to your mice that corrupt the land, and ye shall give glory unto the God of Israel, that he may take his hand from off you, and from off your gods, and from off your land.

Wherefore do ye harden your hearts, as the Egyptians and Pharao hardened their hearts: which when he wrought wonderfully among them, did they not let the people go, and they departed?

Now therefore, make a new cart, and take two milch kine on whom there hath come no yoke, and tie the kine to the cart, and bring the calves home from them.

And take the ark of the Lord, and lay it upon the cart, and put the jewels of gold which ye reward him with for a sin offering, in a coffer by the side thereof, and send it away, that it may go.

And if ye see that he go up by the way of his own coast to Bethsames, then it is he that did us this great evil: If no, we shall know then that it is not his hand that smote us, but it was a chance that happened us.

And the men did even so: And took two kine that gave milk, and tied them to the cart, and kept the calves at home.

And they layed the ark of the Lord upon the cart, and the coffer with the mice of gold, and with the images of their emerodes.

And the kine took the straight way to Bethsames, and went on the straight way: and as they went, lowed, and turned neither to the right hand nor to the left: And the

[1] 'Emerodes' are 'hemorrhoids', but the archaic form may be sufficiently familiar to remain undisturbed.

princes of the Philistines went after them, unto the borders of Bethsames.

And they of Bethsames were reaping their wheat harvest in the valley: And they lift up their eyes, and spied the ark, and rejoiced when they saw it.

And the cart came into the field of one Jehosua, a Bethsamite, and stood still there. There was also a great stone: And they clave the wood of the cart, and offered the kine a burnt offering unto the Lord.

And the Levites took down the ark of the Lord, and the coffer that was with it, wherein the jewels of gold were, and put them on the great stone: And the men of Bethsames sacrificed burnt sacrifices, and offered offerings the same day unto the Lord.

And when the five princes of the Philistines had seen it, they returned to Acaron the same day.

And these are the golden emerodes which the Philistines gave for a sin offering to the Lord: for Asdod one, for Gaza one, for Ascalon one, for Gath one, and for Acaron one.

And gold mice, according to the number of all the cities of the Philistines [belonging] to the five lords, both of walled towns, and of towns unwalled, even unto the great [stone] of Abel, whereon they set down the ark of the Lord unto this day, in the field of Jehosua the Bethsamite.

And he smote of the men of Bethsames, because they had looked in the ark of the Lord, and he slew among the people fifty thousand and three score and ten men: And the people lamented, because the Lord had slain the people with so great a slaughter.

Wherefore the men of Bethsames said: Who is able to stand before this holy Lord God? and to whom shall he go from us?

And they sent messengers to the inhabitants of Kiriathiarim, saying: The Philistines have brought again the ark of the Lord, come ye down and fetch it up to you.

Romans VII

Know ye not brethren (for I speak to they that know the law) how that the law hath power over a man, as long as he liveth?

For the woman which is in subjection to a man, is bound by the law to the man, as long as he liveth: But if the man be dead, she is loosed from the law of the man.

So then if while the man liveth, she couple herself with another man, she shall be counted a wedlock breaker: But if the man be dead, she is free from the law, so that she is no wedlock breaker, though she couple herself with another man.

Even so, ye also my brethren, are dead concerning the law by the body of Christ, that ye could be coupled to another, who is raised from the dead, that we should bring forth fruit unto God.

For when we were in the flesh, the lusts of sin which were by the law wrought in our members, to bring forth fruit unto death.

But now are we delivered from the law, and dead unto it whereunto we were in bondage, that we should serve in newness of spirit, and not in the oldness of the letter.

What shall we say then? Is the law sin? God forbid. Nevertheless, I knew not sin, but by the law: For I had not known lust, except the law had said, thou shalt not lust.

But sin, taking occasion by the commandment, wrought in me all manner of concupiscence. For without the law, sin (was) dead.

I once lived without law: But when the commandment came, sin revived,

And I was dead. And the very same commandment, which was ordained unto life, was found to be unto me an occasion of death.

For sin, taking occasion by the commandment, hath deceived me, and by the same slew (me).

Wherefore the law is holy, and the commandment holy, and just, and good.

Was that then which was good, made death unto me? God forbid. But sin, that sin might appear, by that which was good to work death in me: that sin by the commandment, might be out of measure sinful.

For we know, that the law is spiritual: but I am carnal, sold under sin.

For that which I do, I allow not. For what I would, that do I not: but what I hate, that do I.

If I do now that which I would not, I consent unto the law, that it is good.

Now then, it is not I that do it: but sin that dwelleth in me.

For I know, that in me, that is to say in my flesh, dwelleth no good thing. For to will, is present with me: but I find no means to perform that which is good.

For the good that I would, do I not: But the evil which I would not, that do I.

And if I do that I would not, then is it not I that doth it, but sin that dwelleth in me.

I find then by the law, that when I would do good, evil is present with me.

For I delight in the law of God, after the inward man:

But I see another law in my members, revelling against the law of my mind, and subduing me unto the law of sin, which is in my members.

O wretched man that I am: who shall deliver me from the body of this death?

I thank God through Jesus Christ our Lord. So then,

with the mind I myself serve the law of God: but with the flesh, the law of sin.

Romans VIII

There is then no damnation to them which are in Christ Jesu, which walk not after the flesh, but after the spirit.

For the law of the spirit of life, through Jesus Christ, hath made me free from the law of sin and death.

For what the law could not do, in as much as it was weak through the flesh, God sending his own son, in the similitude of sinful flesh, even by sin, condemned sin in the flesh.

That the righteousness of the law, might be fulfilled in us, which walk not after the flesh, but after the spirit.

For they that are carnal, are carnally minded: But they that are spiritual, are spiritually minded.

To be carnally minded, is death: But to be spiritually minded, is life and peace:

Because that the fleshly mind is enmity against God: For it is not obedient to the law of God, neither can be.

So then, they that are in the flesh, cannot please God.

But ye are not in the flesh, but in the spirit, if so be that the spirit of God dwell in you. If any man have not the spirit of Christ, the same is none of his.

And if Christ be in you, the body is dead because of sin: but the spirit is life for righteousness sake.

But, if the spirit of him that raised up Jesus from the dead, dwell in you: even he that raised up Christ from the dead, shall also quicken your mortal bodies, because that his spirit dwelleth in you.

Therefore brethren, we are debtors, not to the flesh, to live after the flesh.

For if ye live after the flesh, ye shall die: But if ye through the spirit, do mortify the deeds of the body, ye shall live.

For as many as are led by the spirit of God, they are the sons of God.

For ye have not received the spirit of bondage again to fear: but ye have received the spirit of adoption, whereby we cry, Abba, father.

The same spirit, beareth witness to our spirit, that we are the sons of God.

If we be sons, then are we also heirs, the heirs of God, and joint-heirs with Christ: So that we suffer together, that we may be also glorified together.

For I am certainly persuaded that the afflictions of this time, are not worthy of the glory which shall be shewed upon us.

For the fervent desire of the creature, abideth looking when the sons of God shall appear:

Because the creature is subject to vanity, not willing, but for him which hath subdued the same in hope.

For the same creature shall be made free from the bondage of corruption, into the glorious liberty of the sons of God.

For we know, that every creature groaneth with us also, and travaileth in pain, even unto this time.

Not only (they), but we also which have the first fruits of the spirit, and we our selves mourn in ourselves, and wait for the adoption, even the deliverance of our body.

For we are saved by hope: But hope that is seen, is no hope. For how can a man hope for that which he seeth?

But and if we hope for that we see not, then do we with patience abide for it.

Likewise, the spirit also helpeth our infirmities. For we know not what to desire as we ought: but the spirit maketh great intercession for us, with groanings, which cannot be expressed.

And he that searcheth the hearts, knoweth what is the meaning of the spirit: for he maketh intercession for the saints according to the pleasure of God.

For we know that all things work for the best, unto them that love God, to them which also are called of purpose.

For those which he knew before, he also did predestinate, that they should be like fashioned unto the shape of his son, that he might be the first begotten among many brethren.

Moreover, whom he did predestinate, them also he called. And whom he called, them also he justified: And whom he justified, them he also glorified.

What shall we then say to these things? If God be on our side, who can be against us?

Which spared not his own son, but gave him for us all: How shall he not with him also give us all things?

Who shall lay any thing to the charge of Gods chosen? It is God that justifieth:

Who is he that can condemn? It is Christ which died, yea rather which is raised again, which is also on the right hand of God, and maketh intercession for us.

Who shall separate us from the love of God? Shall tribulation or anguish, or persecution, either hunger, either nakedness, either peril, either sword?

As it is written: For thy sake are we killed all day long, and are counted as sheep for the slaughter.

Nevertheless, in all these things we overcome, through him that loved us.

For I am sure, that neither death, neither life, neither angels, nor rule, neither power, neither things present, neither things to come,

Neither height nor depth, neither any other creature, shall be able to separate us from the love of God, which is in Christ Jesu our Lord.

8

DOUAI–RHEIMS

The complete Douai Bible was issued in 1609–10 by Roman Catholic priests in exile. The Rheims New Testament which was its first instalment had already been separately printed at Rheims in 1582; the same college produced both parts, but between 1582 and 1609 it had moved for practical reasons. The translation was based on St Jerome's Latin Bible, in the official Vulgate edition commissioned by the Pope in partial fulfilment of the recommendations of the Council of Trent. The Douai Bible reproduces many of the characteristic qualities of the Latin in an English which is both brilliant and supple. It was the English Bible of Catholics for more than a century, and then through a number of more or less unhappy revisions until the Bible of Mgr Knox, which appeared after the Second World War. The original text of the Douai Bible has not been reprinted in modern times and the original edition is a rare book. It consists of two dumpy quartos in roman type. There was no edition printed in England until the late eighteenth century.

Psalm LXVI

Unto the end, in hymns, a Psalm of Canticle to David

God have mercy upon us, and bless us: illuminate his countenance upon us, and have mercy on us.

That we may know thy way upon earth: in all nations thy salvation.

Let peoples O God, confess to thee: let all peoples confess to thee.

Let nations be glad and rejoice: because thou judgest peoples in equity, and the nations in earth thou doest direct.

Let peoples O God confess to thee, let all peoples confess to thee: the earth hath yielded her fruit.

God, our God bless us, God bless us: and let all the ends of the earth fear him.

Psalm XCII

Praise of Canticle to David himself, in the day before the Sabbath, when the earth was founded

Our Lord hath reigned, he hath put on beauty: our Lord hath put on strength, and hath girded himself.

For he hath established the round world, which shall not be moved.

Thy seat is prepared from that time: thou art from everlasting.

The rivers O Lord have lifted up: the rivers have lifted up their voice.

The rivers have lifted up their waves, above the voices of many waters.

The surges of the sea are marvellous; marvellous is our Lord on high.

Thy testimonies are made credible exceedingly: holiness becometh thy house O Lord for length of days.

Psalm CXXXVIII

Unto the end, a Psalm of David

Lord thou hast proved me, and hast known me: thou hast known me sitting down, and my rising up.

Thou hast understood my cogitations far off: my path, and my cord thou hast searched out.

And thou hast foreseen all my ways: because there is not a word in my tongue.

Behold O Lord thou hast known all the last things, and them of old: thou hast formed me, and hast put thy hand upon me.

Thy knowledge is become marvellous of me: it is made great, and I cannot reach to it.

Whither shall I go from thy spirit? and whither shall I flee from thy face?

If I shall ascend into heaven, thou art there: if I descend into hell, thou art present.

If I shall take my wings early, and dwell in the extreme parts of the sea:

Certes thither also shall thy hand conduct me: and thy right hand shall hold me.

And I said: Perhaps darkness shall tread over me: and the night is mine illumination in my delights.

For darkness shall not be darkened from thee, and the night shall be lightened as the day: as the darkness thereof, so also the light thereof.

Because thou hast possessed my reins: thou hast received me from my mothers womb.

I will confess to thee, because thou art terribly magnified thy works are marvellous, and my soul knoweth exceedingly.

My bone is not hid from thee, which thou madest in secret: and my substance in the lower parts of the earth.

Mine imperfection thine eyes have seen, and in thy book all shall be written: days shall be formed, and no man in them.

But to me thy friends O God are become honourable exceedingly: their principality is exceedingly strengthened.

I will number them, and they shall be multiplied above the sand: I rose up and I am yet with thee.

If thou shalt kill sinners O God: ye men of blood depart from me.

Because you say in thought: they shall receive thy cities in vain.

Did not I hate them, that hate thee O Lord: and pined away because of thine enemies?

With perfect hatred did I hate them: they are become enemies to me.

Prove me O God, and know my heart: examine me, and know my paths.

And see, if the way of iniquity be in me: and conduct me in the everlasting way.

Canticle of Canticles (Song of Songs) 1

Let him kiss me with the kiss of his mouth: because thy breasts are better than wine, smelling fragrantly of the best ointments. Oil poured out is thy name: therefore have young maids loved thee. Draw me: we will run after thee in the odour of thine ointments. The king hath brought me into his cellars: we will rejoice and be glad in thee, mindful of thy breasts above wine: the righteous love thee. I am black but beautiful, o ye daughters of Jerusalem, as the tabernacles of Cedar, as the skins of Salomon. Do not consider me that I am brown, because the sun hath altered my colour: the sons of my mother have fought against me,

they have made me a keeper in the vineyards: my vineyard
I have not kept. Show me o thou, whom my soul loveth,
where thou feedest, where thou liest in the midday, lest I
begin to wander after the flocks of thy companions. If thou
know not thyself, o most fairest among women, go forth,
and follow after the steps of the flocks, and feed thy kids
beside the tabernacles of the shepherds.[1] To my company of
horsemen, in the chariots of Pharao, have I likened thee,
o my love. Thy cheeks are beautiful as the turtledoves, thy
neck as jewels. We will make thee chains of gold, enamelled
with silver. Whiles the king was at his repose, my spikenard
gave the odour thereof. A bundle of myrrh my beloved is to
me, he shall abide between my breasts. A cluster of cypre[2]
my love is to me, in the vineyards of Engaddi. Behold thou
art fair, o my love, behold thou art fair, thine eyes are as of
doves. Behold thou art fair my beloved, and comely: our
little bed is flourishing. The beams of our houses are of
cedar, our rafters of cypress trees.

Canticle of Canticles II

I am the flower of the field, and the lily of the valley. As the
lily among the thorns, so is my love among the daughters.
As the appletree among trees of the woods, so is my beloved
among the sons. Under his shadow, whom I desired, I sat:
and his fruit was sweet unto my throat. He brought me into

[1] I have written 'shepherds' for 'pastours', which is an obsolete form
both of 'pastures' and 'pastors'; the Latin text is *'iuxta tabernacula
pastorum'*.
[2] The plant 'cypre' is an odoriferous Egyptian henna, the Latin is
'botrus cypri'; Wycliffe had first translated it as 'the cluster of cipre tree',
but the Geneva translators, followed by the Authorized Version, call
it 'camphire', which is really a form of camphor, a famous antaphro-
disiac with a bitter taste, inept in this context.

the winecellar, he hath ordered in me charity. Stay me up with flowers, compass me about with apples: because I languish with love. His left hand under my head, and his right hand shall embrace me. I adjure you o daughters of Jerusalem, by the roes, and the harts of the fields, that you raise not, nor make the beloved to awake, until herself will. The voice of my beloved, behold he cometh leaping in the mountains, leaping over the little hills: my beloved is like unto a roe, and to a fawn of harts. Behold he standeth behind our wall, looking through the windows, looking forth by the gates. Behold my beloved speaketh to me: Arise, make haste my love, my dove, beautiful one, and come. For winter is now past, the rain is gone, and departed. The flowers have appeared in our land, the time of pruning is come: the voice of the turtle dove is heard in our land: the figtree hath brought forth her green figs: the flourishing vineyards have given their savour. Arise my love, my beautiful one, and come. My dove in the holes of the rock, in the hollow places of the wall, show me thy face, let thy voice sound in mine ears: for thy voice is sweet, and thy face comely. Catch us the little foxes, that destroy the vineyards: for our vineyard hath flourished. My beloved to me, and I to him, who feedeth among the lilies, till the day break, and the shadows decline. Return: be like, my beloved, to a roe, and to the fawn of harts upon the mountains of Bether.

Canticle of Canticles III

In my little bed in the nights I have sought him, whom my soul loveth, I have sought him, and have not found. I will rise, and will go about the city: by the streets and high ways, I will seek him whom my soul loveth: I have sought him, and have not found. The watchmen which keep the city found me; have you seen him, whom my soul loveth? When I had a little passed by them, I found him whom my soul loveth: I held him: neither will I let him go, till I bring him into my mothers house and into the chamber of her that bare me. I adjure you o daughters of Jerusalem by the roes, and the harts of the fields, that you raise not up, nor make the beloved to awake, till herself will. What is she, that ascended by the desert, as a little rod of smoke of the aromatical spices of myrrh, and frankincense, and of all powder of the apothecary? Behold three score valiants of the most valiant of Israel, compass the little bed of Salomon: all holding swords, and most cunning to battles: every mans sword upon his thigh for fears by night. King Salomon hath made him a portable throne of the wood of Libanus: the pillars thereof he hath made of silver, the seat of gold, the going up of purple: the midst he hath paved with charity for the daughters of Jerusalem. Go forth ye daughters of Sion, and see king Salomon in the diadem, wherewith his mother hath crowned him in the day of his despousing, and in the day of the joy of his heart.

Canticle of Canticles IV

How beautiful art thou my love, how beautiful art thou! thine eyes as it were of doves, besides that, which lyeth hid within. Thy hairs as the flocks of goats, which have come up from mount Galaad. Thy teeth as flocks of them that are shorn, which have come up from the lavatory, all with twins, and there is no barren among them. Thy lips as a scarlet lace: and thy speech sweet. As a piece of a pome-granate, so are also thy cheeks, besides that which lyeth hid within. Thy neck is as the tower of David, which is built with bulwarks: a thousand targets hang on it, all the armour of the valiants. Thy two breasts as two fawns the twins of a roe, which feed among the lilies, till the day aspire, and the shadows decline. I will go to the mount of myrrh, and to the little hill of frankincense. Thou art all fair, o my love, and there is not a spot in thee. Come from Libanus my spouse, come from Libanus, come: thou shalt be crowned from the head of Amena, from the top of Sanir and Hermon, from the dens of lions, from the mountains of leopards. Thou hast wounded my heart, my sister spouse, thou hast wounded my heart in one of thine eyes, and in one hair of thy neck. How beautiful are thy breasts my sister spouse! thy breasts are more beautiful than wine, and the odour of thine ointments above all aromatical spices. Thy lips my spouse are as an honey comb distilling, honey and milk and under thy tongue: and the odour of thy garments as the odour of frankincense. My sister spouse is a garden enclosed, a garden enclosed, a fountain sealed up. Thy offsprings a paradise of pomegranates with orchard fruits. Cypress with spikenard, spikenard, and saffron, sweet cane and cinnamon, with all the trees of Libanus, myrrh and aloes with all the chief ointments. The fountain of gardens: the well of living waters, which run with violence from Libanus. Arise Northwind, and come Southwind, blow through my garden, and let the aromatical spices thereof flow.

Canticle of Canticles v

Let my beloved come into his garden, and eat the fruit of his appletrees. I am come into my garden o my sister spouse, I have reaped my myrrh, with mine aromatical spices: I have eaten the honeycomb with mine honey, I have drunk my wine with my milk: eat o friends, and drink, and be inebriated my dearest. I sleep, and my heart watcheth: the voice of my beloved knocking: Open to me my sister, my love, my dove, mine immaculate: because my head is full of dew, and my locks of the drops of the nights. I have spoiled myself of my robe, how shall I be clothed with it? I have washed my feet, how shall I defile them? My beloved put his hand through the hole, and my belly trembled at his touch. I arose, that I might open to my beloved: my hands have distilled myrrh, and my fingers are full of most approved myrrh. I opened the bolt of my door to my beloved: but he had turned aside, and was passed. My soul melted, as he spake: I sought, and found him not: I called, and he did not answer me. The keepers that go about the city found me: they struck me, and wounded me: the keepers of the walls took away my cloak. I adjure you o daughters of Hierusalem, if you shall find my beloved, that you tell him, that I languish with love. What manner of one is thy beloved of the beloved, o most beautiful of women? What manner of one is thy beloved of the beloved, that thou hast so adjured us? My beloved is white and ruddy, chosen of thousands. His head is as the best gold: his hairs as the branches of palmtrees, black as a raven. His eyes as doves upon the little rivers of waters, which are washed with milk, and sit beside the most full streams. His cheeks are as little beds of aromatical spices set of the pigmentaries. His lips are as lilies distilling principal myrrh. His hands wrought round of gold, full of hyacinths. His belly of ivory, distinguished with sapphires. His thighs as pillars of marble, that are upon feet of gold. His form as of Libanus, erect as the cedars. His throat most sweet, and he whole to be desired: such an one is my beloved, and he is my friend, o daughters of Hierusalem. Whither is thy beloved gone o most beautiful of women? whither is thy beloved turned aside, and we will seek him with thee?

Canticle of Canticles VI

My beloved is gone down into his garden, to the bed of aromatical spices, to feed in the gardens, and to gather lilies. I to my beloved, and my beloved to me, who feedeth among the lilies. Thou art fair O my love, sweet, and comely as Hierusalem: terrible as the army of a camp set in array. Turn away thine eyes from me, because they have made me flee away. Thy hairs as a flock of goats, which have appeared from Galaad. Thy teeth as a flock of sheep, which have come up from the lavatory, all with twins, and there is no barren among them. As the bark of a pomegranate, so are thy cheeks beside what is hidden within thee. There are threescore queens, and fourscore concubines, and of young maids there is no number. My dove is one, my perfect one, she is the only to her mother, elect to her that bare her. The daughters have seen her, and declared her to be most blessed: the queens and concubines, and have praised her. What is she, that cometh forth as the morning rising, fair as the moon, elect as the sun, terrible as the army of a camp set in array? I came down into the garden of nuts, to see the fruits of the valleys and to look if the vineyard had flourished, and the pomegranates budded. I knew not: my soul troubled me for the chariots of Aminadab. Return, return O Sulamitess: return, return that we may behold thee.

Canticle of Canticles VII

What shalt thou see in the Sulamitess but the companies of camps? How beautiful are thy paces in shoes, O princes daughter! the joints of thy thighs are as jewels, that are made by the hand of the artificer. Thy navel as a round bowl, never wanting cups. Thy belly as an heap of wheat, compassed about with lilies. Thy two breasts, as two fawns the twins of a roe. Thy neck as a tower of ivory. Thine eyes as the fishpools in Hesebon, which are in the gate of the daughter of the multitude. Thy nose as the tower of Libanus, that looketh against Damascus. Thy head as Carmelus: and the hairs of thy head as a kings purple tied to conduit pipes. How beautiful art thou, and how comely my dearest, in delights! Thy stature is like to a palmtree, and thy breasts to clusters of grapes. I said: I will go up into the palmtree, and will take hold of the fruits thereof: and thy breasts shall be as the clusters of a vineyard: and the odour of thy mouth as it were of apples. Thy throat as the best wine, worthy for my beloved to drink, and for his lips and his teeth to ruminate.[1] I to my beloved, and his turning is toward me. Come my beloved, let us go forth into the field, let us abide in the villages. Let us rise early to the vineyards, let us see if the vineyard flourish, if the flowers be ready to bring forth fruits, if the pomegranates flourish: there will I give thee my breasts. The Mandragoras[2] have given a smell. In our gates all fruits: the new and the old, my beloved, I have kept for thee.

Canticle of Canticles VIII

Who shall give to me thee my brother, sucking the breasts of my mother, that I may find thee without, and kiss thee,

[1] 'Ruminate' translates '*ad ruminandum*'. 'Ruminant' of an animal seems not to occur until the 1660s.

[2] 'Mandragoras' translates '*mandragorae*'. The narcotic sense of 'mandragora' prevailed from the time of Shakespeare (Gregory Martin was older) but 'mandragora' or 'mandrake' will be found as a desirable fruit at *Genesis* xxx. 14 in Coverdale (1535) and in the Authorized Version, although in the Song of Songs it was driven out by pomegranate. The New English Bible restores 'mandrakes' and makes 'the odour of thy mouth' not that of apples but apricots.

and now no man despise me? I will take hold of thee, and will bring thee into my mothers house: there thou shalt teach me, and I will give thee a cup of spiced wine, and new wine of my pomegranates. His left hand under my head, and his right hand shall embrace me. I adjure you O daughters of Jerusalem, that you raise not up, nor make the beloved to awake till herself will. Who is this, that cometh up from the desert, flowing with delights, leaning upon her beloved? Under the appletree I raised thee up: there thy mother was corrupted, there she was deflowered that bare thee. Put me as a seal upon thy heart, as a seal upon thine arm: because love is strong as death: jealousy is hard as hell, the lamps thereof lamps of fire and flames. Many waters cannot quench charity, neither shall floods overwhelm it: if a man shall give all the substance of his house for love, as nothing he shall despise it. Our sister is little, and hath no breasts. What shall we do to our sister in the day when she is to be spoken unto? If she be a wall, let us build upon it bulwarks of silver: if she be a door, let us join it together with boards of cedar. I am a wall: and my breasts are as a tower, since I was made before him as one finding peace. The peacemaker had a vineyard, in that which hath peoples: he delivered the same to keepers, a man bringeth for the fruit thereof a thousand pieces of silver. My vineyard is before me. A thousand are thy peacemakers, and two hundred for them, that keep the fruits thereof. Thou that dwellest in the gardens, the friends do harken: make me hear thy voice. Flee, O my beloved, and be like to the roe, and to the fawn of harts upon the mountains of aromatical spices.

Wisdom VI

Wisdom is better than strength: and a wiseman[1] than a strong. Hear therefore ye kings, and understand, learn ye judges of the ends of the earth. Give ear ye, that rule multitudes, and that please your selves in multitudes of nations: because the power is given you of our Lord, and strength by the Highest, who will examine your works, and search your cogitations: because when you were the ministers of his kingdom, you judged not rightly, nor kept the law of justice, nor have walked according to the will of God. Horribly and quickly will he appear to you: because most severe judgement shall be done on them, that bear rule. For to the little one mercy is granted: but the mighty shall mightily suffer torments. For God will not except any mans person, neither will fear the greatness of any man: because he made the little and the great, and he hath equally care of all. But to the stronger more strong torment is imminent. To you therefore O kings are these my words, that you may learn wisdom, and not fall. For they that have kept just things justly, shall be justified: and they that have learned these things, shall find what they may answer. Covet ye therefore my words, and love them, and you shall have discipline. Wisdom is clear, and such as never fadeth, and is easily seen of them that love her, and is found of them that seek her. She preventeth them that covet her, that she first may show herself unto them. He that awaketh early to her, shall not labour: for he shall find her sitting at her doors. To think therefore of her, is perfect understanding: and he that watcheth for her, shall quickly be secure. Because she goeth about seeking them that be worthy of her, and in the ways she will show herself to them cheerfully, and in all providence she will meet them.

[1] 'Wiseman' as one word persisted to the generation of Pope.

For the beginning of her is the most true desire of discipline. The care therefore of discipline, is love: and love, is the keeping of her laws: and the keeping of the laws, is the consummation of incorruption: and incorruption maketh to be next to God. Therefore the desire of wisdom leadeth to the everlasting kingdom. If therefore you be delighted with thrones, and with sceptres O ye kings of the people, love wisdom, that you may reign for ever. Love the light of wisdom all ye that bear rule over peoples. But what wisdom is, and how she was made, I will declare: and I will not hide from you the mysteries of God, but from the beginning of her nativity I will search out, and set the knowledge of her into light, and will not let pass the truth: neither will I go with pining envy: because such a man shall not be partaker of wisdom. But the multitude of the wise is the health of the round world: and a wise king is the stability of the people. Therefore take ye discipline by my words, and it shall profit you.

Isaiah 11 1–4

The word, that Isaias the son of Amos saw upon Juda and Jerusalem. And in the later days the mountain of the house of our Lord shall be prepared, in the top of mountains, and it shall be elevated above the little hills: and all nations shall flow unto it. And many peoples shall go, and shall say, come and let us go up to the mount of our Lord, and to the house of the God of Jacob, and he will teach us his ways, and we shall walk in his paths: because the law shall come forth from Sion, and the word of our Lord from Jerusalem. And he shall judge the Gentiles, and rebuke many peoples: and they shall turn their swords into coulters, and their spears into scythes: nation shall not lift up sword against nation, neither shall they be exercised any more to battle.

Isaiah XXIII. 1–11

The burden of Tyre. Howl ye ships of the sea, because the house is destroyed, from whence they were wont to come: from the land of Cethim it is revealed to them. Hold your peace ye that dwell in the isle: the traffickers of Sidon passing over the sea, have replenished thee. The seed of Nilus in many waters, the harvest of the river was her fruits: and she was made the traffic of the nations. Be ashamed Sidon, for the sea sayeth, the strength of the sea, saying: I have not travailed, and I have not brought forth, and I have not nourished young men, nor brought virgins to their growth. When it shall be heard in Egypt, they will be sorry when they shall hear of Tyre: Pass over the seas, howl ye that dwell in the isle. Is not this your city, which gloried from ancient days in her antiquity? her feet shall lead her afar to sojourn. Who hath thought this against Tyre, that was some time crowned, whose merchants were princes, her chapmen the nobles of the earth? The Lord of hosts hath thought it, that he might pluck down the pride of all glory, and bring all the glorious of the earth to ignominy. Pass thy land as a river, O daughter of the sea, thou hast a girdle no more. He hath stretched forth his hand upon the sea, he hath troubled kingdoms.

Isaiah XXIX. 7–10

And the multitude of all nations, that have fought against Ariel, shall be as the dream of a vision in the night, and all that have blasphemed,[1] and besieged and prevailed against it. And as he that is hungry dreameth, and eateth, but when he is awake, his soul is empty: and as he that is thirsty dreameth, and drinketh, and after he is awake, faint as yet thirsteth, and his soul is empty: so shall the multitude be of all the Gentiles, that have fought against Mount Sion. Be astonished, and marvel, waver, and stagger: be ye drunk, and not of wine: be moved, and not of drunkenness. Because our Lord hath mingled unto you the spirit of drowsiness, he will shut your eyes, he will cover your prophets and princes, that see visions.

Isaiah xxx

Woe unto renegade children, saith our Lord, that you would take counsel, and not of me: and would begin a web, and not by my spirit, that you might add sin upon sin: which walk to go down into Egypt, and have not asked my mouth, hoping for help in the strength of Pharao, and having confidence in the shadow of Egypt. And the strength of Pharao shall be a confusion to you, and the confidence of the shadow of Egypt an ignominy. For thy princes were in Tanis, and thy messengers came even to Hanes. All were confounded upon the people, that could not profit them: they were no help, nor to any profit, but to confusion and to reproach. The burden of the beasts of the South. In a land of tribulation and distress, the lioness, and the lion of them, the viper and the flying basiliscus carrying their riches upon the shoulders of beasts, and their

---

[1] I have here written 'blasphemed' for 'waried', a word in common use to mean a deliberate curse in the late Middle Ages and well enough attested throughout the sixteenth; it seems hardly to have survived 1600 except in dialect.

treasures upon the bunch of camels to a people, that cannot be able to profit them. For Egypt shall help in vain, and to no purpose: therefore have I cried upon this: It is pride only, cease. Now therefore going in write to her upon box, and draw it diligently in a book, and it shall be in the latter day for a testimony for ever. For it is a people provoking to wrath, and lying children, children that will not hear the law of God. Which say to the seers: See not: and to them that behold: Behold us not those things that are right: Speak unto us pleasant things, see errors unto us. Take from me the way, turn away the path from me, let the holy one of Israel cease from our face. Therefore thus sayeth the holy one of Israel: For that you have rejected this word and have hoped in calumny and tumult, and have leaned thereupon: therefore shall this iniquity be unto you as a breach that falleth, and is found lacking in a high wall, because suddenly, whiles it is not hoped, shall come the destruction thereof. And it shall be broken small, as the potters vessel is broken with mighty breaking: and there shall not a shred[1] be found of the fragments thereof, wherein a little fire may be carried from the burning, or a little water be drawn out of the pit. Because thus sayeth our Lord the God of Israel: If you return and be quiet, you shall be saved: in silence and in hope shall your strength be. And you would not: and you have said: No, but we will flee to horses: therefore shall you flee. And we will mount upon swift ones: therefore shall they be swifter, that shall persecute you. A thousand men at the face of the terror of one: and at the face of the terror of five shall you flee, till you be least as the mast of a ship in the top of a mountain, and as a sign upon a little hill. Therefore our

---

[1] The word 'shred' is written 'shread', a possible spelling but just possibly a printer's error for 'sheard', a form of 'sherd', which is what might seem to be meant.

Lord expecteth that he may have mercy on you: and therefore shall he be exalted sparing you: because our Lord is
the God of judgement: blessed are all they that expect him.
For the people of Sion shall dwell in Jerusalem: weeping
thou shalt not weep, pitying he will pity thee: at the voice
of thy cry as soon as he shall hear, he will answer thee. And
our Lord will give you strait bread, and short water: and
will not make thy doctor to flee away from thee any more:
and thine eyes shall see thy master. And thine ears shall
hear the word of him, that behind thy back admonisheth
thee: this is the way, walk in it: and decline ye not neither
to the right hand, nor to the left. And thou shalt con-
taminate the plates of the sculptils[1] of thy silver, and the
garment of the molten of thy gold, and shalt scatter them
as the uncleanness of a menstruous woman. Thou shalt say
to it: Get thee hence. And rain shall be given to thy seed,
wheresoever thou shalt sow in the land: and the bread of
the corn of the land shall be most plentiful, and fat. The
lamb in that day shall feed at large in thy possession: and
thine oxen, as the ass colts, that till the ground, shall eat
mingled provender as it was fanned in the floor. And there
shall be upon every high mountain, and upon every little
hill elevated, rivers of running waters in the day of the
killing of many when the towers shall fall. And the light
of the moon shall be as the light of the sun, and the light
of the sun shall be sevenfold, as the light of seven days in
the day, when our Lord shall bind up the wound of his
people, and shall heal the stroke of their wound. Behold
the name of our Lord cometh from far, his burning fury,
and heavy to bear: his lips are filled with indignation, and
his tongue as a devouring fire. His spirit as a torrent over-

[1] 'Sculptil' as a noun translating '*sculptilia*' does occur more than once
in the late Middle Ages, but always in translations of the Latin Bible;
as an adjective it had a renewed life in writers like Sir Thomas Brown.

flowing even to the midst of the neck, to destroy the
nations to nothing, and the bridle of error, that was in the
jaws of peoples. There shall be a song unto you as the night
of a sanctified solemnity, and joy of heart as he that goeth
with a shaulm,[1] to enter into the mount of our Lord to the
strong one of Israel. And our Lord shall make the glory
of his voice to be heard, and shall show the terror of his
arm, in threatening of fury, and flame of devouring fire:
he shall dash to pieces in whirlwind, and in hail stone. For
at the voice of our Lord shall Assur fear being stroken with
the rod. And the passage of the rod shall never cease, which
our Lord shall make to rest upon him in timbrels and harps:
and in principal battles he shall overthrow them. For Topheth
is prepared since yesterday, prepared of the king, deep, and
wide. The nourishments thereof, fire and much wood: the
breath of our Lord as a torrent of brimstone kindling it.

Isaiah LV

All ye that thirst come to the waters: and you that have no
silver, make haste, buy, and eat: come, buy without silver,
and without any exchange wine and milk. Why bestow you
silver not for bread, and your labour not for satiety?
Hearing hear ye me, and eat that which is good, and your
soul shall be delighted in fatness. Incline your ear, and come
to me: hear, and your soul shall live, and I will make an
everlasting covenant with you, the faithful mercies of
David. Behold I have given him for a witness to the peoples,
for a prince and master to the Gentiles. Behold thou shalt
call the nation, which thou knowest not: and the nations
that knew not thee shall run to thee, because of the Lord

[1] The 'shaulm' or 'shawm' was a real instrument, something like an
oboe.

thy God, and the holy one of Israel: because he hath glorified thee. Seek ye our Lord whiles he may be found, invocate him, whiles he is near. Let the impious forsake his way, and the unjust man his cogitations, and return to our Lord, and he will have mercy on him, and to our God: because he is bountiful to forgive. For my cogitations are not your cogitations: nor your ways my ways, sayeth our Lord. For as the heavens are exalted above the earth, so are my ways exalted above your ways, and my cogitations above your cogitations. And as the shower cometh down, and the snow from heaven, and returneth no more thither, but inebriateth the earth, and watereth it, and maketh it to spring, and giveth seed to the sower, and bread to him that eateth: so shall my word be, which shall proceed from my mouth: it shall not return to me void, but it shall do what things soever I would, and shall prosper in these things for which I sent it. Because you shall go forth in joy, and in peace shall you be conducted, the mountains and the little hills shall sing praise before you, and all the wood of the country shall clap the hand. For the shrub, shall come up the fir tree, and for the nettle, shall grow the myrtle tree: and our Lord shall be named for an everlasting sign, that shall not be taken away.

Lamentations of Jeremiah 1

How doth the city full of people, sit solitary: how is the lady of the Gentiles become as a widow: the princess of provinces is made tributary?

Weeping she hath wept in the night, and her tears are on her cheeks: there is none to comfort her of all her dear ones: all her friends have despised her, and are become her enemies.

Judas is gone into transmigration because of affliction,

and the multitude of bondage: she hath dwelt among the Gentiles, neither hath she found rest: all her persecuters have apprehended her within the straits.

The ways of Sion mourn, because there are none that come to the solemnity: all her gates are destroyed: her priests sighing: her virgins loathsome, and herself is oppressed with bitterness.

Her adversaries are made in the head, her enemies are enriched: because our Lord hath spoken upon her for the multitude of her iniquities: her little ones are led into captivity, before the face of the afflicter.

And from the daughter of Sion all her beauty is departed: her princes are become as rams not finding pastures: and they are gone without strength before the face of the pursuer.

Jerusalem hath remembered the days of her affliction, and prevarication of all her things worthy to be desired, which she had from the days of old, when her people fell in the enemies hand, and there was no helper: the enemies have seen her, and have scorned her sabbaths.

Jerusalem hath sinned a sin, therefore is she made unstable: all that did glorify her, have despised her, because they have seen her ignominy: but she sighing is turned backward.

Her filthiness is on her feet, neither hath she remembered her end: she is pulled down exceedingly, not having a comforter: see O Lord mine affliction, because the enemy is exalted.

The enemy hath thrust his hand to all her things worthy to be desired: because she hath seen the Gentiles enter into her sanctuary, of whom thou gavest commandment that they should not enter into thy church.

All her people sighing, and seeking bread: they have given all precious things for meat to refresh the soul, see O Lord and consider, because I am become vile.

O all ye that pass by the way, attend, and see if there be

sorrow like to my sorrow: because he hath made vintage of me, as our Lord hath spoken in the day of the wrath of his fury.

From on high he hath cast a fire in my bones, and hath caught me: he hath spread a net for my feet, he hath turned me backward: he hath made me desolate, all the day consumed with sorrow.

The yoke of mine iniquities hath watched: they are folded together in his hand, and put upon my neck: my strength is weakened: our Lord hath given me into the hand, from which I cannot rise.

Our Lord hath taken away all my magnifical ones out of the midst of me: he hath called a time against me, to destroy mine elect: our Lord hath trodden the winepress to the virgin the daughter of Juda.

Therefore am I weeping, and mine eye shedding tears: because a comforter is made far from me, converting my soul: my children are become desolate because the enemy hath prevailed.

Sion hath spread forth her hands, there is none to comfort her: our Lord hath commanded against Jacob, round about him are his enemies: Jerusalem is become a woman polluted with menstruous flows among them.[1]

Our Lord is just, because I have provoked his mouth to wrath: hear I beseech all ye peoples, and see my sorrow: my virgins, and my young men are gone into captivity.

I have called my friends, they have deceived me: my priests and my ancients are consumed in the city: because they have sought meat for themselves, to refresh their soul.

See O Lord that I am in tribulation, my belly is troubled: my heart is overturned in myself, because I am full of bitterness: the sword killeth abroad, and at home it is like death.

---

[1] The 1609 text reads 'a woman polluted with menstruous floores'; since this is a translation of *'quasi polluta menstruis'* and since 'floores' yields no sense, I have assumed a printer's or copyist's error.

They have heard that I do sigh, and there is none to comfort me: all mine enemies have heard mine evil, they have rejoiced, because thou hast done it, thou hast brought a day of consolation, and they shall be made like to me.

Let all their evil enter in before thee: and vintage them, as thou hast vintaged me for all mine iniquities: for my sighings are many, and my heart is sorrowful.

Baruch III. 24–38

O Israel how great is the house of God, and how great is the place of his possession! It is great, and hath no end: high and unmeasurable. There were the Giants those renowned, that were from the beginning, of big stature, expert in war? These did not our Lord choose, neither found they the way of discipline: therefore did they perish. And because they had not wisdom, they perished through their folly. Who hath ascended into heaven, and taken her, and brought her down from the clouds? Who hath passed over the sea, and found her, and brought her above chosen gold? There is none that can know her ways, nor that can search out her paths: but he that knoweth all things, knoweth her, and hath found her out by his prudence: he that prepared the earth in time everlasting, and replenished it with cattle, and fourfooted beasts: he that sendeth forth light, and it goeth: and hath called it, and it obeyeth him with trembling. And the stars have given light in their watches, and rejoiced: they were called, and they said: here we are: and they have shined to him with cheerfulness, that made them. This is our God, and there shall none other be esteemed against him. He found out all the way of discipline, and delivered it to Jacob his servant, and to Israel his beloved. After these things he was seen upon the earth, and was conversant with men.

Ezechiel XXXVI. 1–11

And thou son of man, prophesy concerning the mountains of Israel, and thou shalt say: Mountains of Israel hear ye the word of our Lord: Thus sayeth our Lord God: For that the enemy hath said of you: Aha, the everlasting heights are given to us for an inheritance: therefore prophesy, and say: Thus sayeth our Lord God: For that you have been desolate, and trodden down round about, and made an inheritance to the rest of the Gentiles, and have ascended upon the lip of the tongue, and the reproach of the people: therefore ye mountains of Israel hear the word of our Lord God: Thus sayeth our Lord God to the mountains, and hills, to the torrents, and valleys, and the deserts, and broken walls, and to the cities forsaken which are spoiled, and scorned of the rest of the Nations round about. Therefore thus sayeth our Lord God: Because in fire of my zeal I have spoken of the rest of the nations, and of all Iduma, which have given my land to themselves for an inheritance with joy, and with all their heart, and with the mind: and have cast it forth to waste it: therefore prophesy concerning the ground of Israel, and thou shalt say to the mountains, and hills, to the hilltops, and valleys: Thus sayeth our Lord God: Behold I have spoken in my zeal, and in my fury because you have sustained the confusion of the Gentiles. Therefore thus sayeth our Lord God: I have lifted my hand, that the Gentiles which are round about you, they may bear their confusion. But you o mountains of Israel may shoot forth your boughs, and bring forth your fruit to my people of Israel: for he is at hand to come. Because lo I to you, and I will turn to you, and you shall be ploughed, and shall take seed. And I will multiply in you men, and all the house of Israel: and the cities shall be inhabited, and the ruinous places shall be repaired. And I will replenish you with men, and with beasts: and they shall be multiplied, and increase: and I will make you dwell as from the beginning, and will endow you with greater gifts, than you have had from the beginning: and you shall know that I am the Lord.

Daniel x

In the third year of Cyrus king of the Persians, a word was revealed to Daniel surnamed Baltassar, and a true word, and great strength: and he understood the word: for there is need of understanding in vision. In those days I Daniel mourned the days of three weeks, desiderable[1] bread I did not eat, and flesh and wine entered not into my mouth, yea neither with ointment was I anointed: till the days of three weeks were accomplished. And in the four and twentieth day of the first month I was by the great river, which is Tigris. And I lifted up mine eyes, and I saw: and behold a man clothed with linen clothes, and his reins girded with the finest gold: and his body as it were the chrysolithus, and his face as the form of lightning, and his eyes as a burning lamp: and his arms, and the parts that are downward even to the feet, as it were the form of glistering brass: and the voice of his word as the voice of a multitude. And I Daniel alone saw the vision: moreover the men that were with me, saw it not, but exceeding terror fell upon them, and they fled away, and hid themselves. And I being left alone saw this great vision: and there remained no strength in me, yea and my shape of countenance was changed in me, and I withered, neither had any strength. And I heard the voice of his words: and hearing I lay astonished upon my

[1] The form 'desiderable' entered English as a translation of biblical Latin in the late Middle Ages, but like a garden escape which becomes native it took root and survived in other contexts until the late seventeenth century, though it was always rare.

face, and my visage cleaved to the ground. And behold a
hand touched me, and lifted me up upon my knees, and
upon the joints of my hands. And he said to me: Daniel
thou man of desires, understand the words, that I speak to
thee, and stand in thy place: for now am I sent to thee.
And when he had said this word to me, I stood trembling.
And he said to me: Fear not Daniel: because since the first
day that thou didst set thy heart to understand to afflict
thyself in the sight of thy God, thy words have been heard:
and I am come for thy words. But the prince of the kingdom
of the Persians resisted me one and twenty days: and behold
Michael one of the chief princes came to aid me, and I
tarried there by the king of the Persians. But I am come to
teach thee what things shall come to thy people in the later
days, because as yet the vision unto days. And when he
spake to me in these manner of words, I cast down my
countenance to the ground, and held my peace. And behold
as it were the similitude of the son of man touched my lips,
and opening my mouth I spake, and said to him, that stood
before me: My lord, in thy vision my joints are dissolved,
and no strength hath remained in me. And how can the
servant of my Lord speak with my Lord? for no strength
is remaining in me, yea and my breath is stopped. Again
therefore there touched me as it were the vision of a man,
and strengthened me, and he said: Fear not O man of
desires, Peace be to thee: take courage and be strong. And
when he spake with me, I received strength, and said:
Speak my Lord, because thou hast strengthened me. And
he said: Doest thou know wherefore I am come to thee?
and now I will return, that I may fight against the prince
of the Persians. When I therefore went forth, there appeared
the prince of the Greeks coming. But yet I will tell thee
that which is expressed in the scripture of truth: and none
is my helper in all these, but Michael your prince.

Amos VIII

These things hath our Lord showed to me: and behold an apple hook. And he said: What seest thou Amos? And I said: An apple hook. And our Lord said to me: The end cometh upon my people Israel: I will add no more to pass them. And the hinges of the temple shall creak in that day, sayeth our Lord God: many shall die: in every place shall silence be cast. Hear this you that tread down the poor, and make the needy of the land to fail, saying: When will the month pass, and we shall sell wares: and the Sabbath, and we open the corn: that we may diminish the measure, and increase the shekel[1] and convey in deceitful balances, that we may for silver possess the needy, and the poor for shoes, and may sell the refuse of the corn. Our Lord hath sworn against the pride of Jacob: If I shall forget even to the end all their works. Why, shall not the land be moved upon this, and every inhabitant thereof mourn: and rise up as a river altogether, and be cast out, and run down to the river of Egypt? And it shall be in that day, sayeth our Lord God: The sun shall go down at midday, and I will make the earth to be dark in the day of light. And I will turn your festivities into mourning, and all your songs into lamentation: and I will bring in upon every back of yours sackcloth, and upon every head baldness: and I will lay it as the mourning of an only begotten son, and the latter end thereof as a bitter day. Behold the days come, sayeth our Lord, and I will send forth famine into the land: not the famine of bread, nor thirst of water, but of hearing the word of the Lord. And they shall be moved from the sea even to sea, and from the North even to the East: they shall go about seeking the word of our Lord, and shall not find. In that day the fair virgins shall fail,

[1] 'Shekel' is given in the text in the old form 'sicle'.

and the youngmen[1] in thirst. They that swear by the sin
of Samaria, and say: Thy God O Dan liveth: and the way of
Bersebee liveth: and they shall fall, and shall rise no more.

2 Machabees VI

But not long after the king sent a certain ancient man of
Antioch, that should compel the Jews to remove themselves from the laws of their fathers and of God: to con-
taminate also the temple that was in Jerusalem, and to call
it by the name of Jupiter Olympius: and in Garizim,
according as they were that inhabited the place, of Jupiter
Hospitalis. And the invasion of the evils was sore and
grievous to all: for the temple was full of the lechery and
gluttony of the Gentiles: and of them that played the
harlots with whores. And women thrusting themselves of
their own accord into the sacred houses, bringing in those
things which were not lawful. The altar also was full of
unlawful things, which were forbidden by the laws. And
neither were the Sabbaths kept, nor the solemn days of the
fathers observed neither plainly did any man confess himself to be a Jew. But they were led with bitter necessity
in the kings birth day to sacrifices: and when the feast of
Bacchus was kept, they were compelled to go about
crowned with Ivy unto Bacchus. And there went forth a
decree into the next cities of the Gentiles, the Ptolomeans
giving the advice, that they also in like manner should do
against the Jews, that they might sacrifice: and them that
would not pass to the ordinances of the heathen, they should
kill. A man then might see the misery. For two women were
accused to have circumcised[2] their children: whom, the

'Youngmen' is divided between lines but hyphenated.
[2] The text gives not 'circumcised' but 'circumcided', an otherwise
unrecorded form in English, which seems to derive from French.

infants hanging at their breasts, when they had openly led them about through the city, they threw down head-long by the walls. And others coming together to the next caves, and secretly keeping the day of the Sabbath, when they were discovered to Philip, were burnt with fire, because they feared for religion and observance, to help themselves with their hand.

But I beseech them that shall read this book, that they abhor not for the adversities, but that they account those things, which have happened, not to be for the destruction, but for the chastening of our stock. For not to suffer sinners a long time to do as they will, but forthwith to punish, is a token of a great benefit. For, not as in other nations our Lord patiently expecteth, that when the day of judgement shall come he may punish them in the fulness of sins: so also doth he determine in us, that our sins being come to the end, so at length he may punish us. For which cause he never certes removeth away his mercy from us: but chastening his people by adversity, he forsaketh them not. But let these things be said of us in few words for an admonition of the readers. And now we must come to the story.

Therefore Eleazarus one of the chief of the Scribes, a man stricken in age, and comely of countenance, with open mouth gaping was compelled to eat swines flesh. But he embracing rather a most glorious death than an hateful life, went before voluntarily to the punishment. And considering how he ought to come patiently sustaining, he determined not to commit unlawful things for love of life. But they that stood by, moved with unlawful pity, for the old friendship of the man, taking him in secret, desired that flesh might be brought, which it was lawful for him to eat, that he might feign to have eaten, as the king had commanded, of the flesh of the sacrifice: that by this fact he might be delivered from death: and for the old friendship of the man, they did him this courtesy. But he began to think upon the worthy pre-eminence of his age and ancientness, and the hoar hairs of natural nobility, and his doings from a child of very good conversation, and according to the ordinances, and the holy law made of God, he answered quickly, saying: that he would rather be sent unto hell. For it is not meet, quoth he, for our age, to feign: that many young men thinking, that Eleazarus of four score year and ten is passed to the life of Aliens: they also through my dissimulation, and for a little time of corruptible life, may be deceived, and hereby I may purchase a stain, and a curse to mine old age. For although at this present time I be delivered from the punishments of men, yet neither alive nor dead shall I escape the hand of the Almighty. Wherefore in departing manfully out of this life, I shall appear worthy of mine old age: and to young men I shall leave a constant example, if with ready mind and stoutly I suffer an honest death, for the most grave and most holy laws. These things being spoken, forthwith he was drawn to execution. And they that led him, and had been a little before more mild, were turned into wrath for the words spoken of him, which they thought were uttered through arrogance. But when he was now in killing with the strokes, he groaned, and said: O Lord, which hast the holy knowledge, thou knowest manifestly that whereas I might be delivered from death, I do sustain sore pains of the body: but according to the soul, for thy fear I do willingly suffer these things. And this man certes in this manner departed this life, leaving not only to young men, but also to the whole nation the memory of his death for an example of virtue and fortitude.

9

THE AUTHORIZED VERSION (1611)

The official Bible of the Church of England, sometimes called King James's Bible, has been immensely influential perhaps since its appearance in 1611 but more certainly since the restoration of monarchy and of the church in 1660. The first edition, now comparatively rare, was a blackletter folio. Small revisions and differences in the text were introduced silently and piecemeal in later editions; by the end of the eighteenth century they may amount to a significant set of alterations; the edition I have used, that of Edinburgh 1803, seemed to me sufficiently close to the original, nor does it differ essentially from modern printings. The 1611 translation was made by a number of scholars, whose names were listed and are known; it was based both on earlier versions and on the original languages; but the personal roles of the scholars, the precise processes of annotation of a basic text with new variants, the collations of versions, and the various revisions that produced the book of 1611 were complicated so that they are only now being studied.

Genesis XXVIII 10–22

And he lighted upon a certain place, and tarried there all night, because the sun set: and he took of the stones of that place, and put them for his pillows, and lay down in that place to sleep.

And he dreamed, and behold a ladder set upon the earth, and the top of it reached to heaven: and behold the angels of God ascending and descending on it.

And, behold, the Lord stood above it, and said, I am the Lord God of Abraham thy father, and the God of Isaac: the land whereon thou liest, to thee will I give it, and to thy seed:

And thy seed shall be as the dust of the earth; and thou shalt spread abroad to the west, and to the east, and to the north, and to the south: and in thee, and in thy seed, shall all the families of the earth be blessed.

And, behold, I am with thee, and will keep thee in all places whither thou goest, and will bring thee again into this land: for I will not leave thee, until I have done that which I have spoken to thee of.

And Jacob awaked out of his sleep, and he said, Surely the Lord is in this place, and I knew it not.

And he was afraid, and said, How dreadful is this place! this is none other but the house of God, and this is the gate of heaven.

And Jacob rose up early in the morning, and took the stone that he had put for his pillows, and set it up for a pillar, and poured oil upon the top of it.

And he called the name of that place Beth-el: but the name of that city was called Luz at the first.

And Jacob vowed a vow, saying, If God will be with me, and will keep me in this way that I go, and will give me bread to eat, and raiment to put on,

So that I come again to my father's house in peace; then shall the Lord be my God.

And this stone, which I have set for a pillar, shall be God's house: and of all that thou shalt give me, I will surely give the tenth unto thee.

Exodus XXVI. 31–7

And thou shalt make a veil of blue, and purple, and scarlet, and fine twined linen, of cunning work: with cherubims shall it be made.

And thou shalt hang it upon four pillars of shittim-wood overlaid with gold: their hooks shall be of gold, upon the four sockets of silver.

And thou shall hang up the veil under the taches,[1] that thou mayest bring in thither within the veil the ark of the testimony: and the veil shall divide unto you between the holy place and the most holy.

And thou shalt put the mercy-seat upon the ark of the testimony in the most holy place.

And thou shalt set the table without the veil, and the candlestick over against the table, on the side of the tabernacle toward the south: and thou shall put the table on the northside.

And thou shalt make an hanging for the door of the tent, of blue, and purple, and scarlet, and fine twined linen, wrought with needle-work.

And thou shalt make for the hanging five pillars of shittim-wood, and overlay them with gold, and their hooks shall be of gold: and thou shalt cast five sockets of brass for them.

1 *Samuel* XX. 30–42

Then Saul's anger was kindled against Jonathan, and he said unto him, Thou son of the perverse rebellious woman, do not I know that thou hast chosen the son of Jesse to

---

[1] A 'tache' is a broad-headed nail; the word had existed since the fifteenth century, and was still in use up to fifty years after 1611.

thine own confusion, and unto the confusion of thy mother's nakedness?

For as long as the son of Jesse liveth upon the ground, thou shalt not be established, nor thy kingdom: wherefore now send and fetch him unto me: for he shall surely die.

And Jonathan answered Saul his father, and said unto him, Wherefore shall he be slain? What hath he done?

And Saul cast a javelin at him to smite him: whereby Jonathan knew that it was determined of his father to slay David.

So Jonathan arose from the table in fierce anger, and did eat no meat the second day of the month: for he was grieved for David, because his father had done him shame.

And it came to pass in the morning, that Jonathan went out into the field at the time appointed with David, and a little lad with him.

And he said unto his lad, Run, find out now the arrows which I shoot. And as the lad ran, he shot an arrow beyond him.

And when the lad was come to the place of the arrow which Jonathan had shot, Jonathan cried after the lad, and said, Is not the arrow beyond thee?

And Jonathan cried after the lad, Make speed, haste, stay not. And Jonathan's lad gathered up the arrows, and came to his master.

But the lad knew not anything: only Jonathan and David knew the matter.

And Jonathan gave his artillery unto his lad, and said unto him, Go, carry them to the city.

And as soon as the lad was gone, David arose out of a place toward the south, and fell on his face to the ground, and bowed himself three times; and they kissed one another, and wept one with another, until David exceeded.

And Jonathan said to David, Go in peace, forasmuch as

we have sworn both of us in the name of the Lord, saying, The Lord be between me and thee, and between my seed and thy seed for ever. And he arose and departed: and Jonathan went into the city.

1 Kings 1. 22–48

And, lo, while she yet talked with the king, Nathan the prophet also came in.

And they told the king, saying, Behold Nathan the prophet. And when he was come in before the king, he bowed himself before the king with his face to the ground.

And Nathan said, My Lord, O king, hast thou said, Adonijah shall reign after me, and he shall sit upon my throne?

For he is gone down this day, and hath slain oxen, and fat cattle, and sheep in abundance, and hath called all the king's sons, and the captains of the host, and Abiathar the priest: and, behold, they eat and drink before him, and say, God save king Adonijah.

But me, even me thy servant, and Zadok the priest, and Benaiah the son of Jehoiada, and thy servant Solomon, hath he not called.

Is this thing done by my lord the king, and thou hast not shewed it unto thy servant, who should sit on the throne of my lord the king after him?

Then king David answered and said, Call me Bathsheba: and she came into the king's presence, and stood before the king.

And the king sware, and said, As the Lord liveth, that hath redeemed my soul out of all distress,

Even as I sware unto thee by the Lord God of Israel, saying, Assuredly Solomon they son shall reign after me, and he shall sit upon my throne in my stead; even so will I certainly do this day.

Then Bath-sheba bowed with her face to the earth, and did reverence to the king, and said, Let my lord king David live for ever.

And king David said, Call me Zadok the priest, and Nathan the prophet, and Benaiah the son of Jehoiada. And they came before the king.

The king also said unto them, Take with you the servants of your lord, and cause Solomon my son to ride upon mine own mule, and bring him down to Gihon:

And let Zadok the priest, and Nathan the prophet, anoint him there king over Israel: and blow ye with the trumpet, and say, God save king Solomon.

Then ye shall come up after him, that he may come and sit upon my throne; for he shall be king in my stead: and I have appointed him to be ruler over Israel and over Judah.

And Benaiah the son of Jehoiada answered the king, and said, Amen: the Lord God of my lord the king say so too.

As the Lord hath been with my lord the king, even so be he with Solomon, and make his throne greater than the throne of my lord king David.

So Zadok the priest, and Nathan the prophet, and Benaiah the son of Jehoiada, and the Cherethites, and the Pelethites, went down, and caused Solomon to ride upon king David's mule, and brought him to Gihon.

And Zadok the priest took an horn of oil out of the tabernacle, and anointed Solomon: and they blew the trumpet; and all the people said, God save king Solomon.

And all the people came up after him; and the people piped with pipes, and rejoiced with great joy, so that the earth rent with the sound of them.

And Adonijah, and all the guests that were with him, heard it as they had made an end of eating. And when Joab heard the sound of the trumpet, he said, Wherefore is this noise of the city being in an uproar?

And while he yet spake, behold, Jonathan, the son of Abiathar the priest, came: and Adonijah said unto him, Come in; for thou art a valiant man, and bringest good tidings.

And Jonathan answered and said to Adonijah, Verily our lord king David hath made Solomon king.

And the king hath sent with him Zadok the priest, and Nathan the prophet, and Benaiah the son of Jehoiada, and the Cherethites, and the Pelethites, and they have caused him to ride upon the king's mule:

And Zadok the priest, and Nathan the prophet, have anointed him king in Gihon; and they are come up from thence rejoicing, so that the city rang again. This is the noise that ye have heard.

And also Solomon sitteth on the throne of the kingdom.

And moreover, the king's servants came to bless our lord king David, saying, God make the name of Solomon better than thy name, and make his throne greater than thy throne: and the king bowed himself upon the bed.

And also thus said the king, Blessed be the Lord God of Israel, which hath given one to sit on my throne this day, mine eyes even seeing it.

1 Kings II. 1–11

Now the days of David drew nigh that he should die; and he charged Solomon his son, saying,

I go the way of all the earth: be thou strong therefore, and shew thyself a man;

And keep the charge of the Lord thy God, to walk in his ways, to keep his statutes, and his commandments, and his judgements, and his testimonies, as it is written in the law of Moses, that thou mayest prosper in all that thou doest, and whithersoever thou turnest thyself;

That the Lord may continue his word, which he spake concerning me, saying, If thy children take heed to their way, to walk before me in truth with all their heart, and with all their soul, there shall not fail thee (said he) a man on the throne of Israel.

Moreover, thou knowest also what Joab the son of Zeruiah did to me, and what he did to the two captains of the hosts of Israel, unto Abner the son of Ner, and unto Amasa the son of Jether, whom he slew, and shed the blood of war in peace, and put the blood of war upon his girdle that was about his loins, and in his shoes that were on his feet.

Do therefore according to thy wisdom, and let not his hoar head go down to the grave in peace.

But shew kindness unto the sons of Barzillai the Gileadite, and let them be of those that eat at thy table: for so they came to me when I fled because of Absalom thy brother.

And, behold, thou hast with thee Shimei the son of Gera, a Benjamite of Bahurim, which cursed me with a grievous curse in the day when I went to Mahanaim: but he came down to meet me at Jordan, and I sware to him by the Lord, saying, I will not put thee to death with the sword.

Now therefore hold him not guiltless; for thou art a wise man, and knowest what thou oughtest to do unto him; but his hoar head bring thou down to the grave with blood.

So David slept with his fathers, and was buried in the city of David.

And the days that David reigned over Israel were forty years: seven years reigned he in Hebron, and thirty and three years reigned he in Jerusalem.

Job, xxxvii

At this also my heart trembleth, and is moved out of his place.

Hear attentively the noise of his voice, and the sound that goeth out of his mouth.

He directeth it under the whole heaven, and his lightning unto the ends of the earth.

After it a voice roareth: he thundereth with the voice of his excellency; and he will not stay them when his voice is heard.

God thundereth marvellously with his voice: great things doeth he, which we cannot comprehend.

For he saith to the snow, Be thou on the earth; likewise to the small rain, and to the great rain of his strength.

He sealeth up the hand of every man; that all men may know his work.

Then the beasts go into dens, and remain in their places.

Out of the south cometh the whirlwind; and cold out of the north.

By the breath of God frost is given; and the breadth of the waters is straitened.

Also by watering he wearieth the thick cloud: he scattereth his bright cloud,

And it is turned round about by his counsels; that they may do whatsoever he commandeth them upon the face of the world in the earth.

He causeth it to come, whether for correction, or for his land, or for mercy.

Hearken unto this, O Job: stand still, and consider the wondrous works of God.

Dost thou know when God disposed them, and caused the light of his cloud to shine?

Dost thou know the balancings of the clouds, the wondrous works of him which is perfect in knowledge?

How thy garments are warm, when he quieteth the earth by the south wind?

Hast thou with him spread out the sky, which is strong, and as a molten looking-glass?

Teach us what we shall say unto him; for we cannot order our speech by reason of darkness.

Shall it be told him that I speak? If a man speak, surely he shall be swallowed up.

And now men see not the bright light which is in the clouds; but the wind passeth, and cleanseth them.

Fair weather cometh out of the north: with God is terrible majesty.

Touching the Almighty, we cannot find him out: he is excellent in power, and in judgement, and in plenty of justice: he will not afflict.

Men do therefore fear him: he respecteth not any that are wise of heart.

Job XXXVIII

Then the Lord answered Job out of the whirlwind, and said,

Who is this that darkeneth counsel by words without knowledge?

Gird up now thy loins like a man; for I will demand of thee, and answer thou me.

Where wast thou when I laid the foundations of the earth? declare, if thou hast understanding.

Who hath laid the measures thereof, if thou knowest? or who hath stretched the line upon it?

Whereupon are the foundations thereof fastened? or who laid the corner-stone thereof,

When the morning-stars sang together, and all the sons of God shouted for joy?

Or who shut up the sea with doors, when it brake forth, as if it had issued out of the womb?

When I made the cloud the garment thereof, and thick darkness a swaddling-band for it,

And brake up for it my decreed place, and set bars and doors,

And said, Hitherto shalt thou come, but no further; and here shall thy proud waves be stayed?

Hast thou commanded the morning since thy days; and caused the day-spring to know his place;

That it might take hold of the ends of the earth, that the wicked might be shaken out of it?

It is turned as clay to the seal; and they stand as a garment.

And from the wicked their light is withholden, and the high arm shall be broken.

Hast thou entered into the springs of the sea? or hast thou walked in the search of the depth?

Have the gates of death been opened unto thee? or hast thou seen the doors of the shadow of death?

Hast thou perceived the breadth of the earth? declare if thou knowest it all.

Where is the way where light dwelleth? and as for darkness, where is the place thereof,

That thou shouldest take it to the bound thereof, and that thou shouldest know the paths to the house thereof?

Knowest thou it, because thou wast then born? or because the number of thy days is great?

Hast thou entered into the treasures of the snow; or hast thou seen the treasures of the hail,

Which I have reserved against the time of trouble, against the day of battle and war?

By what way is the light parted, which scattereth the east wind upon the earth?

Who hath divided a watercourse for the overflowing of waters; or a way for the lightning of thunder;

To cause it to rain on the earth, where no man is; on the wilderness, wherein there is no man;

To satisfy the desolate and waste ground; and to cause the bud of the tender herb to spring forth?

Hath the rain a father? or who hath begotten the drops of dew?

Out of whose womb came the ice? and the hoary frost of heaven, who hath gendered it?

The waters are hid as with a stone, and the face of the deep is frozen.

Canst thou bind the sweet influences of Pleiades, or loose the bands of Orion?

Canst thou bring forth Mazzaroth in his season? or canst thou guide Arcturus with his sons?

Knowest thou the ordinances of heaven? canst thou set the dominion thereof in the earth?

Canst thou lift up thy voice to the clouds, that abundance of waters may cover thee?

Canst thou send lightnings, that they may go, and say unto thee, Here we are?

Who hath put wisdom in the inward parts? or who hath given understanding to the heart?

Who can number the clouds in wisdom? or who can stay the bottles of heaven,

When the dust groweth into hardness, and the clods cleave fast together?

Wilt thou hunt the prey for the lion, or fill the appetite of the young lions,

When they couch in their dens, and abide in the covert to lie in wait?

Who provideth for the raven his food? when his young ones cry unto God, they wander for lack of meat.

Job xxxix

Knowest thou the time when the wild goats of the rock bring forth? or canst thou mark when the hinds do calve?

Canst thou number the months that they fulfil? or knowest thou the time when they bring forth?

They bow themselves, they bring forth their young ones, they cast out their sorrows.

Their young ones are in good liking, they grow up with corn; they go forth, and return not unto them.

Who hath sent out the wild ass free? or who hath loosed the bands of the wild ass?

Whose house I have made the wilderness, and the barren land his dwellings.

He scorneth the multitude of the city, neither regardeth he the crying of the driver.

The range of the mountains is his pasture, and he searcheth after every green thing.

Will the unicorn be willing to serve thee, or abide by thy crib?

Canst thou bind the unicorn with his band in the furrow? or will he harrow the valleys after thee?

Wilt thou trust him, because his strength is great? or wilt thou leave thy labour to him?

Wilt thou believe him, that he will bring home thy seed, and gather it into thy barn?

Gavest thou the goodly wings unto the peacocks? or wings and feathers unto the ostrich?

Which leaveth her eggs in the earth, and warmeth them in the dust.

And forgetteth that the foot may crush them, or that the wild beast may break them.

She is hardened against her young ones, as though they were not her's; her labour is in vain without fear;

Because God hath deprived her of wisdom, neither hath he imparted to her understanding.

What time she lifteth up herself on high, she scorneth the horse and his rider.

Hast thou given the horse strength? hast thou clothed his neck with thunder?

Canst thou make him afraid as a grasshopper? the glory of his nostrils is terrible.

He paweth in the valley, and rejoiceth in his strength: he goeth on to meet the armed men.

He mocketh at fear, and is not affrighted; neither turneth he back from the sword.

The quiver rattleth against him, the glittering spear and the shield.

He swalloweth the ground with fierceness and rage; neither believeth he that it is the sound of the trumpet.

He saith among the trumpets, Ha, ha! and he smelleth the battle afar off, the thunder of the captains, and the shouting.

Doth the hawk fly by thy wisdom, and stretch her wings toward the south?

Doth the eagle mount up at thy command, and make her nest on high?

She dwelleth and abideth on the rock, upon the crag of the rock, and the strong place.

From thence she seeketh the prey, and her eyes behold afar off.

Her young ones also suck up blood: and where the slain are, there is she.

Lo now, his strength is in his loins, and his force is in the navel of his belly.

He moveth his tail like a cedar: the sinews of his stones are wrapped together.

His bones are as strong pieces of brass; his bones are like bars of iron.

He is the chief of the ways of God: he that made him can make his sword to approach unto him.

Surely the mountains bring him forth food, where all the beasts of the field play.

He lieth under the shady trees, in the covert of the reed, and fens.

The shady trees cover him with their shadow; the willows of the brook compass him about.

Behold, he drinketh up a river, and hasteth not: he trusteth that he can draw up Jordan into his mouth.

He taketh it with his eyes; his nose pierceth through snares.

Job XL

Moreover, the Lord answered Job, and said,

Shall he that contendeth with the Almighty instruct him? he that reproveth God, let him answer it.

Then Job answered the Lord, and said,

Behold, I am vile; what shall I answer thee? I will lay mine hand upon my mouth.

Once have I spoken, but I will not answer; yea, twice, but I will proceed no further.

Then answered the Lord unto Job out of the whirlwind, and said,

Gird up thy loins now like a man: I will demand of thee, and declare thou unto me.

Wilt thou also disannul my judgement? wilt thou condemn me, that thou mayest be righteous?

Hast thou an arm like God? or canst thou thunder with a voice like him?

Deck thyself now with majesty and excellency, and array thyself with glory and beauty.

Cast abroad the rage of thy wrath; and behold every one that is proud, and abase him.

Look on every one that is proud, and bring him low; and tread down the wicked in their place.

Hide them in the dust together, and bind their faces in secret.

Then will I also confess unto thee that thine own right hand can save thee.

Behold now behemoth, which I made with thee; he eateth grass as an ox.

Job XLI.

Canst thou draw out leviathan with an hook? or his tongue with a cord which thou lettest down?

Canst thou put an hook into his nose? or bore his jaw through with a thorn?

Will he make many supplications unto thee? will he speak soft words unto thee?

Will he make a covenant with thee? wilt thou take him for a servant for ever?

Wilt thou play with him as with a bird? or wilt thou bind him for thy maidens?

Shall thy companions make a banquet of him? shall they part him among the merchants?

Canst thou fill his skin with barbed irons? or his head with fishspears?

Lay thine hand upon him, remember the battle, do no more.

Behold, the hope of him is in vain: shall not one be cast down even at the sight of him?

None is so fierce that dare stir him up: who then is able to stand before me?

Who hath prevented me, that I should repay him? whatsoever is under the whole heaven is mine.

I will not conceal his parts, nor his power, nor his comely proportion.

Who can discover the face of his garment? or who can come to him with his double bridle?

Who can open the doors of his face? his teeth are terrible round about.

His scales are his pride, shut up together as with a close seal.

One is so near to another, that no air can come between them.

They are joined one to another, they stick together, that they cannot be sundered.

By his sneezings[1] a light doth shine, and his eyes are like the eyelids of the morning.

Out of his mouth go burning lamps, and sparks of fire leap out.

Out of his nostrils goeth smoke, as out of a seething-pot or cauldron.

His breath kindleth coals, and a flame goeth out of his mouth.

In his neck remaineth strength, and sorrow is turned into joy before him.

---

[1] The text had 'neesings', of which the usual spelling was 'neezings' for 'sneezings'; Wycliffe had translated this passage with the same word, but it died out during the seventeenth century.

The flakes of his flesh are joined together: they are firm in themselves; they cannot be moved.

His heart is as firm as a stone; yea, as hard as a piece of the nether millstone.

When he raiseth up himself, the mighty are afraid: by reason of breakings they purify themselves.

The sword of him that layeth at him cannot hold; the spear, the dart nor the habergeon.

He esteemeth iron as straw, and brass as rotten wood.

The arrow cannot make him flee; sling-stones are turned with him into stubble.

Darts are counted as stubble: he laugheth at the shaking of a spear.

Sharp stones are under him: he spreadeth sharp-pointed things upon the mire.

He maketh the deep to boil like a pot; he maketh the sea like a pot of ointment.

He maketh a path to shine after him; one would think the deep to be hoary.

Upon earth there is not his like, who is made without fear.

He beholdeth all high things: he is a king over all the children of pride.

Ephesians v. 1–14

Be ye therefore followers of God, as dear children;

And walk in love, as Christ also hath loved us, and hath given himself for us an offering and a sacrifice to God for a sweet-smelling savour.

But fornication, and all uncleanness, or covetousness, let it not be once named among you, as becometh saints;

Neither filthiness, nor foolish talking, nor jesting, which are not convenient; but rather giving of thanks.

For this ye know, that no whoremonger, nor unclean person, nor covetous man, who is an idolater, hath any inheritance in the kingdom of Christ and of God.

Let no man deceive you with vain words: for because of these things cometh the wrath of God upon the children of disobedience.

Be not yet therefore partakers with them.

For ye were sometimes darkness, but now are ye light in the Lord: walk as children of light;

(For the fruit of the Spirit is in all goodness, and righteousness, and truth;)

Proving what is acceptable unto the Lord.

And have no fellowship with the unfruitful works of darkness, but rather reprove them.

For it is a shame even to speak of those things which are done of them in secret.

But all things that are reproved are made manifest by the light: for whatsoever doth make manifest is light.

Wherefore he saith. Awake thou that sleepest, and arise from the dead, and Christ shall give thee light.

10

HUGH BROUGHTON (1662)

Almost all Hugh Broughton's translations of parts of the Bible were posthumously published in 1662. He had suggested a complete new Bible as early as 1593; he was a learned and eccentric Hebrew scholar who did not work on the 1611 Bible, of which when it appeared he bitterly disapproved; he died in 1611. His own collected works, including his translations, were edited in 1662 by John Lightfoot as *The Works of the Great Albionean Divine Mr Hugh Broughton*.

Job XXXVII

Also at this mine heart quaketh: and skippeth out of his place.

Hearken well to the noise of his voice: and to the sound that cometh from his mouth.

He directeth it under the whole heaven: and his light unto the wings of the earth.

After the light, roareth a voice: He thundreth with the voice of his Majesty: He will not have it to be behind, when his voice is to be heard.

The Omnipotent thundreth wonderfully by his voice: he doth great things which we cannot know.

For, to the snow he saith, be upon the earth, or to showers of rain: then showers of much great rain come.

That sealeth up the hand of Adam's son, to peruse what all his workmen may do.

Then the beasts go into their dens: and keep in their lodgings.

A tempest cometh from his chamber, the fair-weather winds.

By the breath of the Omnipotent he giveth ice: and the breadth of the waters are made hard.

So by clearness he wearieth thick-vapours, he scattereth the clouds by his light.

And for varieties, he turneth himself in his wise counsels, for their operation, for whatsoever he commandeth them, in the face of the world, on the earth.

Whether for a scourge, or for the earth, or for mercy, he doth cause it to come.

Give ear unto this O Job, stand still, and consider the wonderous works of the Omnipotent.

Dost thou know when the Puissant disposeth of them, how the light of his cloud doth shine.

Dost thou know the piecing of his thick-vapours: the miracles of the perfect in all knowledge.

How thy clothes are warm; (when the land is still) from the south.

Couldst thou make a firmament with him of the air, settled as glass molten.

Teach us what we should say unto him, we cannot reason for darkness.

Shall it be recorded unto him when I speak, would any plead when he should be undone?

And now men cannot look upon the light, when it is bright in the air, when a wind passeth and cleareth it.

Through the North a golden cometh: but a terrible glory is in the Puissant.

The Almighty, whom we cannot find out, he is huge of

strength: but of judgement and greatness of justice he would not afflict.

Therefore sad men do fear him. He respecteth no wise in heart.

Job XXXVIII

Then answered the Eternal unto Job, out of the whirlwind, and said.

What a man is this, that darkeneth counsel by words void of knowledge.

Gird now thy loins like a man, and I will question with thee: and let me see thy skill.

Where wast thou, when I laid the foundation of the earth, tell if thou know understanding.

Who set her measures? for thou wilt be skilful: or who hath stretched the line upon it?

Whereupon are her foundations sunk fast? or who hath cast her corner stone?

When the morning stars rejoiced together: and all the sons of God shouted.

When he shut up the sea with doors, when it gushed out coming from the womb.

When I set a cloud his garment: and obscurity his swaddling-band.

And brake the earth for it by my decree: and set bar and doors.

And said, Hitherto thou shalt come, but shalt go no farther: and here shall be an end for the pride of thy waves.

Hast thou since thy days given the morning his charge? and hast taught the dawning his place?

To hold the wings of the earth, that the wicked might be shaken out of it.

That it should be made diverse as clay to the pictured, and things stand upon it as a garment.

That the wicked should be restrained of their light, and the arm lift up should be broken.

Camest thou ever to the springs of the sea, or hast thou walked in the border of the deep?

Have the gates of death been opened unto thee? or hast thou seen the gates of the shadow of death?

Hast thou perceived the breadth of the earth? tell if thou knowest it all.

Where is the way that light dwelleth? and where is the place of darkness?

That thou mayest take it into his border, and know the paths of his house.

Didst thou know, that then thou wast to be born, and the number of thy days to be many?

Hast thou come to the storehouse of snow? or hast thou seen the storehouse of hail?

Which I spare unto the time of distress, against the day of battle and war?

By what way is light parted; and the eastwind scattereth itself over the earth?

Who divided a channel for the streams, and a way for the lightning of thunder?

To rain upon the earth where no man is, upon the desert, where none of Adam dwelleth.

To satisfy the waste and vast-ground, and to cause the bud of herb to spring forth.

Hath the rain a father, or who begat the mizzling of dew?

From whose womb came the Ice, and who begat the frost of heaven?

That the waters hide themselves like a stone, and the face of the deep is fastened.

Canst thou bind the delicacies of Pleiades, or loose the bands of Orion?

Canst thou bring forth Mazaroth in due season? Canst thou lead Arcturus and her children?

Dost thou know the rules of heaven, or canst thou set his force upon earth?

Canst thou lift up thy voice unto the clouds, that abundance of water cover thee?

Canst thou send forth the lightnings, that they go, and say to thee, here we are?

Who hath set wisdom in the reins, or who hath given the heart understanding?

Who could make the air Saphir-like by wisdom, or distill the barrels of the heavens?

Sprinkling the dust with this sprinkling, that the clods cleave together?

Job xxxix

Canst thou hunt prey for the hardy-Lion, or satisfy the herds of Lions whelps?

When they couch in their lodge, and tarry in their covert to lie in wait.

Who could prepare for the raven his food, when his young ones cry unto the Omnipotent, they wandering without meat?

Canst thou know the time when the wild goats bring forth young? canst thou mark when hinds calve?

Canst thou number the months that they must fulfil? Canst thou know the time when they bring forth young?

They lie down, they calve their young ones, and pass their travail.

Their young ones wax strong, they grow in the fields, they go forth, and return not unto them.

Hugh Broughton (*1662*)

Who set the wild ass at liberty, or who loosed the bands of that Arad?

Even I, who made the plain wilderness his house, and the barren land his dwelling.

He scorneth the multitude of the city, and will not hear the cry of the driver.

Chosen places in the mountains are his pasture, and he will seek after every green herb.

Will the unicorn do thee service, or will he abide by thy crib?

Canst thou bind the unicorn for the furrow, by his cords? will he plough the valley after thee?

Mayest thou trust him, because his strength is great, or leave thy labour unto him?

Mayest thou believe him, that he will bring home thy corn, or gather it unto thy barn?

Couldest thou give the proud wing to the peacock, or feather to the stork, and ostrich?

Which leaveth her eggs in the ground, and warmeth them in the dust:

And forgetteth how a foot may dash them, and the beasts of the field may tread upon them.

So hard she is to her own young ones, as though they were not hers, and had laboured in vain without fear.

Because the Puissant hath denied her wisdom, and not given her understanding.

At what time it mounteth on high; she scorns the horse and his rider.

Canst thou give to the horse courage? Canst thou clothe his neck with thundering?

Canst thou make him quake as a locust, or his proud snorting[1] with terror?

[1] For 'snorting' Broughton has 'snurting'; this excellent word was in use from the fifteenth century until about Broughton's time, but it has survived only in dialect.

His feet will dig in the plain ground, he rejoiceth in his strongness, he will go forth to meet the harness.

He mocks terror, and shrinketh not, neither starteth back from the sword:

Though the quiver rattle upon him, with bright blade, with spear with javelin.

With shaking and stirring he beateth upon the earth, and will not stand still at the voice of the trumpet.

Of the trumpet he will say, Heah, and from far will smell the battle, the thunder and shout of princes.

Doth the Hawk flee from thy wisdom, spreading the wings toward the south?

Mounts the Eagle on high by thy mouth, or doth it make the nest on high?

He dwelleth and lodgeth on a rock, in the edge of a rock, and a fortress.

Then he searcheth meat, his eyes will see far off.

His young near choke swallowing blood, and where carcases be, resort they.

Job XL

Moreover the Eternal spake to Job, and said:

Who is the pleader that will check the Omnipotent? let the reprover of the puissant speak to any one of these things.

Then Job answered the Eternal, and said:

Lo, I am vile, what shall I answer thee, I will lay my hand on my mouth.

Once I spake, but I will not answer, or twice, but I will no more.

Then the Eternal answered Job out of the whirlwind, and said:

Gird now thy loins like a man, and I will question with thee, and let me see thy skill.

Wilt thou disanul my judgement, condemn me that thou mayest be just?

Or hast thou an arm as the Omnipotent? Canst thou thunder with voice as he?

Deck thee now with gayness and height, and put on glory and honour.

Cast abroad wrath of thine anger, and behold each proud, and humble him.

Behold each proud, make him bow down; beat wicked to dust as they stand.

Hide them in the dust together, bind their faces in the hid place.

And then I will confess to thee; that thy right hand can save thee.

Behold now Behemoth, which I have made with thee, he eateth grass as an ox:

Behold now his strength is in his loins, and his power in the navel of his belly.

He will make his tail stand like a Cedar: the sinews of his stones are plaited in and out as branches.

His bones be as bars of steel; his hard parts as staves of iron.

He is the chief of the Omnipotents ways: He that made him, dare join his sword.

The mountains do bring him fodder: where all the field beasts play boldly.

He resteth him in the shadow, in the covert of reed and fens.

Shade places cover him with their shade, the willows rivers cover him.

Lo, he robs a river, that it haste not, he durst think that Jordan would gush into his mouth.

Can men take him before his eyes, to pierce his nose with many snares?

Job XLI

Canst thou draw Leviathan with an hook, or deep a cord into his tongue?

Canst thou put a rush into his nose, or bore his jaw through with a thorn?

Will he make much praying to thee, or speak unto thee tenderly?

Will he make a covenant with thee, that thou take him a servant for ever?

Wilt thou play with him as with a bird? Wilt thou tie him for thy young girls?

Will companions make cheer of him? Shall he be parted to merchants?

Wilt thou fill his skin with sharp-hooks, and his head with fishers angles?

Lay thine hand upon him, look for war, do it no more.

When hope of him proveth false; yea at his very sight one would be cast down.

None is so hardy that dare stir him, and then who can stand before me?

Who gave me anything first, that I may pay it to him again? whatsoever is under the heaven is mine.

I will not keep silence, concerning his members, and speech of strength, and grace of his frame.

Who can uncover the face of his garment? Who can come with his double bridle?

Who dare open the doors of his face? Terror is about his teeth.

The strong shields have pride, he is closed with a strait seal.

One toucheth another so near, that no wind can come betwixt them.

Each doth cleave unto his fellow, hold one the other, and cannot be sundered.

Hugh Broughton (1662)

His sneezing[1] maketh a light shine, and his eyes are like the eyelids of the morning.

Out of his mouth do lamps proceed, and sparks of fire leap of themselves.

From his nostrils issueth a smoke, as a pans or cauldrons seething.

His breath would set coals on fire, and a flame issueth from his mouth.

In his neck doth strength always lodge, and before him danceth carefulness.

The pieces of his flesh cleave fast, hard in him, that none can be moved.

His heart is so hard as a stone, so hard as the nether millstone.

At his stateliness the mighty fear, and of shivering purge themselves.

The sword of one that doth strike him, spear, dart and javelin, will not fasten.

He holds iron as straw, and steel as rotten wood.

The bows child drives him not away, the sling stones turn as chaff to him.

The axes are counted as chaff, and he will laugh at shaking spikes.

His underneath places be as a sharp shards; he spreads the pricking in the mire.

He makes the deep boil as a pot, sets the sea as a spicers kettle.

After him he makes the way lighten, and thinks the sea to be hoary.

His like are not upon the land, which do deal without fear.

He despiseth all lofty things: he is King over all the wild kind.

[1] For 'sneezing' Broughton has 'neising'.

Job XLII

Then Job answered the Eternal, and said:

I know thou canst do all things, and no wisdom was kept from thee.

What a man hath this been, who hides counsel without knowledge; Therefore I tell, that I had not understanding: wonders are above me, such I know not.

O hear me, when I do speak, I will make petition unto thee, and teach thou me.

By ear hearing I heard of thee, but now mine eye hath seen thee.

Therefore I loathe myself, and I will repent in dust and ashes.

Now after the Eternal had spoken these words unto Job, the Eternal said to Eliphaz the Themanite, I am displeased with thee, and thy two friends, for ye have not spoken of me the right, as my servant Job.

But now take to you seven oxen, and seven rams, and go to my servant Job: and offer a burnt offering for yourselves, and my servant Job shall pray for you. For certainly I will accept his person, that I punish not your foolishness, where ye have not spoken the right of me, as my servant Job.

So went they, Eliphaz the Themanite, and Bildad the Shuchite, and Sophar the Naamathite, and did as the Eternal spake unto them; and the Eternal accepted the person of Job.

And the Eternal restored that which had been taken from Job, when he had prayed for his friends: and the Eternal increased all that Job had to double.

Then came to him all his brethren and all his sisters, and all that had been of his acquaintance afore, and did eat bread with him in his house: and solaced him, and comforted him, for all the harm which the Eternal had brought upon him. And they gave him each one a lamb, and one ear-ring of gold.

So the eternal blessed the end of Job, more then his beginning: and he had fourteen thousand sheep, and six thousand camels, and a thousand yoke of oxen, and a thousand asses.

And he had seven sons and three daughters.

And he called the name of the first Jemimah, and the name of the second Cassia, and the name of the third, Keren-Happuc.

And no woman-kind was found so fair as the daughters of Job in all the land: And their father gave them inheritance among their brethren.

And Job lived after this, an hundred and forty years, and saw his children, and his childrens children, four generations.

And Job died aged, and full of days.

Ecclesiastes XII

Therefore remember thy Creator in the days of thy youth, before the evil days come, and the years approach, of which thou wilt say, I have no pleasure in them.

Before the Sun is dark, and the light, and the Moon, and the Stars, and the clouds return after the rain.

When the keepers of the house shall tremble, and the strong men shall bow themselves, and the grinders shall cease because they are few, and they wax dark, that look out by the windows.

And the doors shall be shut by the street, with the base sound of the grinding, and a man shall stand up at the voice of the bird, and all the daughters of Music shall be brought low.

And men will dread every high place, and fears will be in the way, and the Almond tree will flourish, and the Grasshopper will be a burden to itself, and all lust will be dissolved, and a man goeth unto his long home; and mourners go about in the street.

Before the silver cord is loosed, and the golden ewer broken, and the pitcher burst at the well, and the wheel broken at the cistern.

And dust return to the earth as it was, and the spirit return to God that gave it.

Vanity of Vanities, saith Koheleth, all is vanity.

And this is a matter of excellency, as Koheleth was wise, still he taught the people knowledge and weighed, and examined, and fitted many Parables:

Koheleth studied to find words delightful, and Scripture rightful words of truth.

The words of the wise; as goades, and nailes fastened in the sheep-folds: being given from one shepherd.

And my son give all diligent heed to them. There is no end in making many books: and much reading is a weariness of the flesh.

The sum of the matter is, all being heard: Fear God and keep his Commandments. For this is all the man.

For God will bring every deed unto judgement; with every hid thing, whether it be good or evil.

Daniel v

Belshazar the King made a great feast to his Nobles, a thousand, and drank Wine before the thousand.

Belshazar commanded for taste of wine, to bring the golden and silver vessels which his father Nebuchadnezar took from the Temple in Jerusalem, that the King, and his

Nobles, his Wives, and his Concubines might drink in them.

Then were brought the golden vessels that were taken from the Temple of the Lords house in Jerusalem, and the King, and his Nobles, his Wives, and his Concubines, drank in them.

They drank wine, and praised the gods of gold, and of silver, of brass, of iron, of wood, and of stone.

At the same hour came forth fingers of a mans hand, and wrote over against the Candlestick upon the plaster of the wall of the kings palace. And the king saw the piece of the hand that wrote.

Then the Kings countenance was changed, and his thoughts troubled him, and the joints of his loines were loosed, and his knees knocked one the other.

The King cried aloud, that they should bring the Astrologians, Chaldeans, and Entrail-lookers. The King spake, and said to the Sages of Babel: Whosoever can read this writing, and show me the interpretation thereof, shall wear Purple, and a chain of gold about his neck, and shall rule the third in the kingdom.

Then came all the Kings Sages, but they could not read the writing, and make known to the King the interpretation of it.

Then was the King Belshazar greatly troubled, and his countenance was changed in him, and his Nobles were amazed.

The Queen, by reason of the Kings words and his Nobles, came into the banquet house. The Queen spake, and said. O King, live for ever: let not thy thoughts trouble thee, and let not thy countenance be changed:

There is a man in thy kingdom, in whom is the spirit of the holy gods, and in the days of thy Father, light and skill, and wisdom, like the wisdom of the gods was found in him: and the King Nebuchadnezar thy Father, made him Provost of the Enchanters, Astrologians, Chaldeans, Entrail-lookers: the King thy Father.

Because an excellent spirit, and knowledge, and skill, the expounding of dreams, and showing of riddles, and dissolving of knotty things were found in him: in Daniel to whom the King gave the name Belteshazar: Now let Daniel be called, and he will show the interpretation.

Then was Daniel brought before the king: The King spake and said to Daniel: Art thou that Daniel, of the children of the captivity of Jehude, whom my father the King brought out of Jehude?

Indeed I have heard of thee, that the spirit of the gods is in thee, and that light, and skill, and excellent wisdom, was found in thee.

And now there hath been brought before me Sages, Astrologians, to read this writing, and to make known to me the interpretation of it, but they could not show the interpretation of the matter.

But I have heard of thee, that thou canst make interpretations, and dissolve knotty things. Now if thou canst read the writing, and make known unto me the interpretation of it, thou shalt wear Purple, and a chain of gold about thy neck, and shalt rule the third in the kingdom.

Then Daniel answered, and said before the King, keep thy gifts to thyself, and give thy rewards to another. But I will read the writing to the King, and make known to him the interpretation.

O King, God the most high gave a kingdom, and greatness, and glory, and honour to Nebuchadnezar thy father.

And for the greatness which he gave him, all people, nations and tongues, trembled and were afraid of him. Whom he would he killed, and whom he would he saved, and whom he would he set up, and whom he would he put down.

But when his heart became haughty, and his spirit was hardened in pride, he was brought down from his royal throne, and they took glory from him.

And he was driven from the sons of man, and joined his heart to the beasts, and had his dwelling with the wild asses, they made him eat grass as the Oxen, and his body was wet with the dew of heaven, until he knew that the high God ruleth over the kingdom of men, and setteth on it whom he will.

And thou his son Belshazar, hast not humbled thy heart, though thou knewest all this.

But hast lift up thyself against the Lord of heaven, and they have brought the vessels of his house before thee: and thou, and thy nobles, thy wives and thy concubines, have drunk wine in them, and hast praised gods of silver and gold, brass, iron, wood, and stone, which see not, nor hear, nor understand. But thou didst not honour God, in whose hand thy breath standeth, and whose are all thy ways.

Then the piece of a hand was sent from before him, and this Scripture written.

And this is the Scripture which is written, MENE, MENE, TEKEL, U-PARSIN.

This is the interpretation of the matter: MENE. God hath numbered thy kingdom, and finished it.

TEKEL, thou art weighed in the balance, and art found wanting.

PERES, thy kingdom is parted, and given to Madai and Paras.

Then commanded Belshazar, and they clothed Daniel with purple, and a chain of gold about his neck, and made a proclamation concerning him, that he should bear rule the third in the kingdom.

The same night was Belshazar King of the Chaldeans slain. And Darius Madai received the kingdom, being about three score and two years old.

II

JOHN CARRYL (1700)

John Carryl's version of the psalms is a simple Roman Catholic translation from the Latin Vulgate for private use, printed in France in contemporary English several times around the year 1700. It has the interest of its unusual origin, and of the rarity of biblical translation in the English of those years; it may not be a great masterpiece but it has interesting virtues of language.

Psalm LXVI

May God be merciful to us and bless us, May the light of his countenance shine upon us, and may he be merciful to us.

That we may know thy way upon the earth, And that thy saving mercy may be made known to all nations.

Let the people praise thee, O God! Let all people praise thee.

Let the nations be glad, Let them be fill'd with joy, For thou judgest the people with equity, and dost rule the nations upon the earth.

Let the people praise thee, O God! Let all people praise thee; The earth has yielded its fruit.

May God, our God, give us his blessing; May God give us his blessing, and may the whole earth fear him from one end to the other.

John Carryl (1700)

Psalm XXII

Our Lord governs me; nothing will be wanting to me, he has put me into a place of excellent pasture.

He has led me to waters of refreshment, he has revived my soul.

He has conducted me in the paths of justice, for the glory of his name.

Should I walk in the middle of the shade of death, I would fear no harm, because thou art with me.

Thy rod, and thy staff have been a comfort to me.

Thou hast prepared, and set before me a table, to strengthen me against those who persecute me.

Thou hast poured oil upon my head, and my inebriating cup how admirable is it?

And thy mercy will accompany me, all the days of my life.

That I may dwell for ever in the house of our Lord.

EDWARD HARWOOD'S
NEW TESTAMENT (1768)

Edward Harwood's *Liberal Translation* of the New Testament, which appeared in 1768, is definitely a freak; the book is not often found and was never so popular as to be reissued; it is a version very much of its time, but freakish even then, not in the free and vigorous English of Johnson, nor in the strong, rhetorical English of a writer like Tom Paine, but in the curious idiom of mid-eighteenth-century high-mindedness, a language neither elegant nor authentic, but florid and riddled with the clichés of the day; it is a habit of speech usually encountered only on tombstones, and is essentially middle class and middlebrow. There are many modern analogies to this style of translation; it is therefore some consolation that Mr Harwood has been forgotten.

Matthew xxv. 31–43

At the last day the Messiah shall descend, invested with matchless splendour and majesty, with a bright and numerous retinue of his angels—and then shall ascend a most magnificent throne.

Before this tribunal all the nations of the universe shall be convened in one vast assembly—these he will then separate into two distinct companies, in the same manner as a shepherd selects and divides the sheep and goats into two separate flocks.

The good he will place on his right hand—the bad on his left.

The judge will then address himself to those on his right hand with smiles of approbation—Welcome! ye blessed of my father! Welcome to the everlasting possession of those blissful abodes, which have from all eternity been prepared for your reception.

For when I was fainting with hunger, you gave me food —when I was parched with thirst, you gave me drink— under your roof, when I was a stranger, I found an hospitable reception.

When I was languishing under cold and nakedness, you cloathed me—when I was sick and helpless, you took the charge of me—when I was confined in prison, you visited me.

The righteous, alarmed at such an unexpected discourse, will then answer—Blessed Messiah! when did we ever see thee languishing with hunger, or fainting with thirst, and in these extremities relieved thee?

When did we ever see thee a forlorn and unhappy stranger, and entertained thee—or indigent and naked, and cloathed thee?

Or when did we ever see thee confined to a sick bed, or to a loathsome dungeon—and in that helpless condition visited and befriended thee?

To this the judge will answer—Since you have done these kind and benevolent offices to the most inconsiderable christian—I consider them as done to myself.

Afterwards the judge will turn to those on his left hand, and say to them, with stern looks, full of indignation— Depart you cursed from my presence, to be consumed in that eternal fire, that was prepared for the devil and his angels.

For tho' I was expiring with hunger and thirst, you repulsed me from your doors.

Tho' I was in a strange country and in distress, you had the cruelty to refuse me the least relief—when you saw me shiver and languish under cold and nakedness—when you saw me rendered helpless by indisposition, or confined in a prison—you neglected me, and left me to all the cruel rigours of my condition.

Luke XXIII

The whole assembly, being unanimously resolved upon his condemnation, conducted him to Pilate the procurator of Judæa.

Soon as they were admitted, they began to alledge many heavy crimes against him—This person, they said, hath been for a number of years seducing the province from their allegiance—using all his influence to prohibit the payment of tribute to the Emperor, and arrogantly stiling himself Messiah the King.

Pilate then said to him, Dost thou assume the title of the sovereign of the Jews?—Jesus answered in the affirmative.

Pilate after examining him, turned to the high priests and to the populace and said—I do not find this man guilty of any capital crime.

At this declaration of the governor they raised loud and vehement clamours—This impostor, they said, hath been raising disturbances in every part of Judæa—haranguing the mob every where—and the tumults he first excited in Galilee have reached the capital and produced universal confusion in the nation.

Upon the mention of Galilee, the procurator asked, if the prisoner was a Galilæan.

And when he understood that the scene of these public transactions had been chiefly laid in Herod's dominions—he ordered him to be conducted to that monarch—whom the present festival had brought to the city.

At the sight of Jesus Herod was in raptures—He had been extremely desirous a long time to see one, of whom he had heard so many amazing accounts—He therefore now flattered himself that his curiosity would be gratified by seeing him perform some signal and astonishing miracle.

He therefore begged and importuned him with repeated and urgent solicitations to favour him with the exhibition of his miraculous power—But to all these importunate entreaties Jesus answered not a word.

The high priests and Jewish clergy stood by all the time, with extreme virulence and incessant clamour charging him with the most atrocious crimes—and vehemently urging his condemnation.

Herod finding his hopes disappointed, looked upon him as an object of the vilest contempt—and himself and his officers joined in insulting and treating him with the lowest banter and derision—After having been the sport of their inhumanity and cruelty they arrayed him in a robe of mock royalty—and sent him back to Pilate.

That day friendship and harmony were restored between Pilate and Herod—and all the former differences that had before subsisted between them, were now composed by a mutual reconciliation.

When Jesus was sent back without any sentence being pronounced upon him by Herod, the procurator convoked the high priests, the magistrates, and the people,

and thus spoke—You have brought before me a person, as a disturber of government, and I have taken an examination of him before you all, but have found him guilty of none of those crimes with which you have charged him.

Neither doth Herod think, tho' he hath heard all that you have alledged against him, that he hath done any thing that merits capital punishment.

I will therefore sentence him to be whipped—and then release him.

For the procurator had established a custom of gratifying them every passover with the acquittal of any one prisoner they should desire—

The whole assembly hearing this—with a loud and violent vociferation cried—Drag him away, Drag him away! and oblige us with the release of Barabbas.

This Barabbas was a notorious ruffian, who had been imprisoned for raising an insurrection in the city, and committing murder.

Pilate desirous to acquit Jesus made a second effort to appease the enraged multitude.

But his voice was drowned in one vehement and universal clamour, that repeated, Crucify him! Crucify him!

He persisted to make a third attempt to placate their violent fury—endeavouring to convince them of their injustice—What capital crime, he asked them, do you charge him with—I have examined him and found nothing in his conduct that deserves death—I will give orders for his being publickly whipped, and dismiss him.

At this they again pierced the air with their cries—and with more determined vehemence and fury than ever demanded his crucifixion—The violence of the populace and the urgent solicitations of the high priests at last prevailed upon the procurator to comply.

Pilate then gave orders that he should be executed according to their request.

At their united importunity he released out of prison one who had perpetrated murder and caused a riot—but surrendered up Jesus to their implacable and bloody resentments.

As they were dragging him to the place of crucifixion they seized one Simon a citizen of Cyrenè, whom they happened to meet as he was coming to the city,—and compelled him to take the cross and carry it after him.

There followed him to the place of execution a prodigious crowd of people—the women beating their breasts and deploring his unhappy fate with the most piercing lamentations.

To these he turned and thus spoke—Ye daughters of Jerusalem! let not my miserable end provoke your tears, but let them flow for the dreadful destiny in which yourselves and your children will shortly be involved.

For the time will soon come, when the distracted mother shall exclaim—Happy, Happy is the barren woman! Thrice happy the bosom that never felt maternal tenderness!

Such dire misery and horror will then reign, that men shall passionately wish the mountains and hills to overwhelm them, and to hide them from the dreadful spectacle.

For if the *green* bough burns with such violence, with what horrid fury will the *dry* tree blaze!

Two malefactors were also conducted along with him to the place of crucifixion.

Being arrived at Calvary, the place of execution, they crucified him between two criminals.

When Jesus was extended on the cross he devoutly uttered this petition to God—Merciful father! grant them thy forgiveness, for they know not what they do!—The soldiers parted his cloaths and cast lots for them.

The common people stood spectators of this whole transaction—among whom were also the principal members of the Sanhedrim—who all united in offering him the most contemptuous insult and abuse—crying out—Since he is the great Messiah, the distinguished favourite of heaven, let him who hath saved such numbers from death, now save himself!

The Roman guards also conjoined in making him the object of their sport and derision—advancing up to his cross, and offering him vinegar,

and insolently saying to him—Since thou art the great sovereign of Judæa, let us see thee rescue thyself from thy present misery.

Over his head they fixed up this inscription in Greek, Latin and Hebrew: THIS IS THE KING OF THE JEWS.

One of the criminals too from his cross calumniated him and said—Since thou art the illustrious Messiah, why dost not thou extricate both thyself and us from our present tortures!

But the other reproved him for his profane insolence, and said to him—How canst thou, who art in the same condemned and wretched circumstances, allow thyself to guilty of such impiety against God!

We indeed justly suffer that punishment which our crimes have merited—but this person hath been guilty of no irregularity.

He then said to Jesus—Do remember me when thou arrivest in thy happy future kingdom!

Jesus said to him—Wretched as I this day am, yet I can assure thee that thou shalt share with me the happiness of a blessed immortality.

At twelve o'clock the whole land of Judæa was enveloped in universal darkness—which continued in all its horrors till three in the afternoon.

The sun was a great blank in the midst of heaven—the veil that separated the sanctuary and the holy of holies was rent in two.

Jesus then with a strong and vehement voice cried out—
O Father! into thy merciful hands I will resign my spirit!—
Having uttered these words he expired.

When the Roman officer saw the *uncommon* circumstance
that attended his last moments, he was struck with religious
awe and reverence, and said—Undoubtedly this was a good
man!

And all the people who were present seeing the amazing
phænomena with which his death was attended, in an
ecstasy of astonishment and horror struck their breasts, and
returned to their respective homes.

All his friends too, and the women who had attended
him in his late journey from Galilee to the city, stood at
some distance, and were spectators of those wonderful
events.

There was at that time a member of the Sanhedrim, whose
name was Joseph—a person of a virtuous and most amiable
character.

He was a native of Arimathea—one who lived in
expectation of the speedy establishment of the Messiah's
kingdom—and who had discovered the greatest aversion
and abhorrence of the procedures of the Jews in this whole
transaction.

This person came to Pilate, and begged he would give
him the body of Jesus.

Having obtained his request, he took down the corpse—
swathed it in fine linen, according to the Jewish custom—
and reposited it in a tomb, which he had very lately hol-
lowed for himself in the solid rock, and in which nobody
had ever been interred.

The next day was called the *Preparation*—being the day
that preceded the Jewish sabbath.

The women, who had accompanied him from Galilee,
followed the body—saw him perform these pious offices,

and remarked the tomb, and the manner in which the corpse was deposited.

After they had seen these funeral obsequies performed—they returned into the city, and purchased a great quantity of rich aromatic spices, intending to embalm him—but deferred it till the sabbath was past—which they kept according to the prescription of the law.

John 1

Before the origin of this world existed the LOGOS—who was then with the Supreme God—and was himself a divine person.

He existed with the Supreme Being, before the foundation of the earth was laid:

For this most eminent personage did the Deity solely employ in the formation of this world, and of every thing it contains.

This exalted spirit assumed human life—and from his incarnation the most pure and sacred emanations of light were derived to illuminate mankind:

This light shot its beams into a benighted world—and conquered and dispelled that gloomy darkness, in which it was inveloped.

To usher this divine personage into the world, and to prepare men for his reception, God previously commissioned and sent John the Baptist.

This prophet came to give public notice that a glorious light would shortly appear—to excite all the Jews to credit and receive this great messenger of God.

John himself openly disavowed all pretensions to this exalted character—declaring, that *he* was only appointed of God to give public information of this illustrious personage.

Epistle to the Romans v

We heathens therefore, having been acquitted from all our prior guilt, in consequence of our sincere belief of Christianity, are now in a state of peace and friendship with the Deity, by means of our Lord Jesus Christ:

Through whom we have been admitted, by our cordial reception of his gospel, into this gracious dispensation, with which we are now blessed, and exult in the glorious prospect of a blessed immortality.

And what is more than this, we even exult and glory in the miseries and distresses we encounter—persuaded that distress produceth constancy:

and constancy produceth self-approbation, and self-approbation hope.

And this animating hope will not result in shameful disappointment, for the love of God to us hath been diffused in our bosoms by the holy Spirit, which hath been imparted to us.

For when we Gentiles were totally unable to extricate ourselves—in this important crisis, Jesus died for the benefit of an impious and immoral race.

For scarcely could any person be found, who would sacrifice his life for a just person—though perhaps some person might generously devote his life a victim, to save a benevolent man from death.

But the Deity exhibiteth a most amazing and endearing expression of his affection for us, that when we were profligate and abandoned sinners, Christ voluntarily submitted to death to save us from destruction.

How much more, therefore, since we have in the present state been acquitted from our vices, by means of the effusion of his blood, shall we in a future state be rescued through him from everlasting perdition!

For if, when we Gentiles were enemies to God, we were introduced into this happy change of state, by means of the *death* of his own son—how much more, having been graciously favoured with this happy revolution, shall we not obtain everlasting salvation by means of that immortal *life* he now enjoys!

And not only this, but we exult and glory in the Deity, on account of the interposition of our Lord Jesus Christ—by whose means we heathens have received this glorious revolution.

In respect to this, as by one man sin was first introduced into the world, and death was ushered in by sin, and, in this manner, death universally invaded the whole human race, in consequence of their universal guilt.

For before the period of the mosaic institution, vice had an existence in the world—though it did not expose men to such rigorous punishments before the publication of that law.

But death exercised its dread dominion through all that long space which intervened betwixt Adam and Moses—over those, who had not violated a positive law, as Adam, the forerunner of the Messiah, had done.

But the disadvantages incurred by the lapse of the *first*, won't admit the least comparison with the free donation of blessings conferred by the *second,* Adam—for if through the disobedience of one person, the human race was subjected to mortality; infinitely more hath the divine benignity, and that liberal grant of gospel privileges, bestowed through the benevolence of one man, Jesus Christ, superabounded to mankind.

Neither in this respect are the effects of Adam's guilt to be placed in opposition with the gracious benefits derived from the gospel-dispensation—For Adam's *single* offence, by the judicial sentence of God, terminated in the *condem-*

nation of the whole human species to mortality—but the gracious privileges of the gospel, taking their origin from the *numerous* vices of the world, have resulted in a total *absolution* of them.

For if, through the single lapse of one person, the universal empire of death was immediately erected—infinitely more shall they, who are blessed with this exuberance of divine goodness, and with the free and generous remission of all their vices, reign in endless immortality through one divine personage, Jesus Christ.

As therefore, in consequence of one sole act of disobedience, all the human race was sentenced to mortality—so in consequence of one sole constitution, are all the human race judicially adjudged to immortality.

For as on the account of the disobedience of one single person, all mankind were treated as sinners—so, on account of the obedience of one single person, shall all mankind be treated as if they were perfectly free from guilt.

But the law of Moses was introduced among but an inconsiderable portion of mankind; so that the violations of that positive law were multiplied without end—but where vice abounded, the immense exuberance of the divine benignity hath infinitely more superabounded:

in order, that as the empire of sin was erected, and scattered mortality among the human race; so in like manner might the divine favour most triumphantly reign unto eternal life, by means of those privileges which were dispensed by Jesus Christ our Lord.

13

BENJAMIN FRANKLIN (1779)

Job 1. 6–11

And it being *levée* day in heaven, all God's nobility came to court, to present themselves before him; and Satan also appeared in the circle, as one of the ministry.

And God said to Satan, You have been some time absent; where were you? And Satan answered I have been at my country-seat, and in different places visiting my friends.

And God said, Well, what think you of Lord Job? You see he is my best friend, a perfectly honest man, full of respect for me, and avoiding every thing that might offend me.

And Satan answered, Does your Majesty imagine that his good conduct is the effect of mere personal attachment and affection?

Have you not protected him, and heaped your benefits upon him, till he is grown enormously rich?

Try him;—only withdraw your favor, turn him out of his places, and withhold his pensions, and you will soon find him in the opposition.

14

WILLIAM BARNES (1859)

This is one of a numerous series of tiny pamphlets simul-
taneously published in 1859, commissioned by the English
Dialect Society. William Barnes was already known as a
poet in Dorset dialect and a serious theorist on linguistic
questions. All the pamphlets were versions of the Song of
Songs, all based on the Authorized Version, which it is
interesting to observe must have ranked as a controlling
text in standard English. The version by Barnes has never
been reprinted and is hard to come by; it deserves to rank
among his poems, and no one who values those poems will
find this version hard to take seriously. The pamphlet
contains a few short pages of notes on Dorset dialect which
I have not reproduced.

The Zong o' Solomon (*Song of Songs* 1)

The zong o' zongs, that is Solomon's.

Let en kiss me wi' the kisses ov his mouth: vor your love
is better than wine.

Vor the smell o' your sweet-smellën scents, shed scent
is your neäme, an' therevore the maïdens do love you.

O draw me on wi' thee, we'll run: the king brought me
into his cheämmer: in you we'll be blissom an' glad, we'll
meäke mwore o' your love than o' wine, the true-hearted
shall love you.

I be zwa'thy, Jerusalem maïdens, but comely, as the black tents of Kedar, as Solomon's hangèns.

Don't watch me, because I be zwa'thy, an' the zun have a-burnt me so dark: the sons o' my mother wer all a-burnt wi' me; they meäde me a keeper o' vineyards; my own vineyard I never kept.

Tell where, O belov'd o' my soul, you do veed, an' do meäke your vlock rest at the noon: that I midden be a-hemm'd in by the vlocks o' your fellors.

If you do know not o' yourzelf, O feäirest o' women, goo out by the tracks o' the vlock, a-veedèn your kids by the tents o' the shepherds.

To a ho'se in a chariot o' Pharaoh I've a-liken'd you, O my belov'd.

Your cheäks be comely wi' beads, an' your neck wi' your chaïns.

We'll meäke vor ye chaïns all o' goold, wi' studs all o' zilver.

While the king is a-zot on his couch, my spiknard do gi'e out its smell.

A bundle o' myrrh is my sweetheart to me; he shall lie all the night in my breast.

My sweetheart to me is a cluster o' camphire in the vineyards ov En-ge-di.

Behold, you be feäir, my belov'd; you be feäir; your eyes be lik' culvers.

Behold, you be feäir, my belov'd, ah! sweet: an' leafy's our bed.

The beams ov our house be o' cedar, our refters o' vir.

Song of Songs II

I be the rwose o' Sharon, an' the lily o' the valleys.

Lik' a lily wi' thorns, is my love among maïdens.

Lik' an apple-tree in wi' the trees o' the wood, is my love among sons. I long'd vor his sheäde, an' zot down, an' his fruit wer vull sweet to my teäste.

He brought me into the feäst, an' his flag up above me wer love.

Refresh me wi' ceäkes, uphold me wi' apples: vor I be a-pinèn vor love.

His left hand wer under my head, an' his right a-cast round me.

I do warn ye, Jerusalem's da'ters, by the roes an' the hinds o' the vield, not to stir, not to weäke up my love, till he'd like.

The vaïce o' my true-love! behold, he's a-comèn; a-leäpèn up on the mountains, a-skippèn awver the hills.

My true-love is lik' a young roe or a hart: he's a-standèn behind our wall, a-lookèn vwo'th vrom the windors, a-showèn out droo the lattice.

My true-love he spoke, an' he call'd me, O rise up, my love, my feäir maïd, come away.

Vor, lo, the winter is awver, the raïn's a-gone by.

The flowers do show on the ground; the zong o' the birds is a-come, an' the coo o' the culver's a-heärd in our land.

The fig-tree do show his green figs, an' the vines out in blooth do smell sweet. O rise up, my true-love, feäir-maïd, come away.

O my love's in the clefts o' the rocks, in the lewth o' the cliffs. Let me look on your feäce, let me heär 'tis your vaïce; vor sweet is your vaïce, an' comely your feäce.

O catch us the foxes, the young oones, a-spweilèn the vines; vor the vines ha'neesh grapes.

O my love is all mine, an' I be all his: he's a-veedèn among the lilies.

Till the day is a-broke, an' the sheädes be a-vled, turn

209

back, O my love, an' be lik' a roe or young hart on the mountains o' Bether.

Song of Songs III

By night on my bed I sought him I do love to my soul: I sought en, but noowhere could vind en; I called en, but he never heärd me.

I'll rise then, an' goo round the town, in the streets, in the squares, a-seekèn the oone I do love to my soul: I sought en, but noowhere could vind en.

The watchmen a-keepèn the town then voun' me: an' I cried, Did ye see the belov'd o' my soul?

I'd only a-left em a-while, when I vound the belov'd o' my soul: I held en, nor let en goo on, till I brought en back into the house o' my mother, the cheämmer ov her that ha' bore me.

I do warn ye, Jerusalem's da'ters, by the roes, by the hinds o' the vields, not to stir, not to weäke up my love, till he'd like.

Who's a-comèn on out o' the wilderness, up lik' a pillar o' smoke, a-smellèn o' myrrh an' o' frankincense, all the sweet scents o' the marchant?

Look at the bed that is Solomon's; round en be dreescore o' warriors, the mighty ov Israel.

They've all ov em swords, an' be all skill'd in war: ev'ry man got hes swoord 'pon hes thigh, becaze of feer in th' night.

King Solamun maade hisself a char-yut of th' wud of Libanon.

He maade th' pellars of et of selver, the bottom of et of gowld, th' cov'rin' of et of poorple, th' middle of et bein' paaved weth love, fur th' dafters of J'rusalum.

William Barnes (*1859*)

Go foathe, Aw you dafters of Zion, and behowld King Solamun weth th' crown weth which hes mother crowned un in the day of hes espousals, and in th' day of th' gladness of hes heart.

Song of Songs IV

Behowld, thee'rt feer, my love; behowld, thee'rt feer; thee'st doves' eyes wethin tha locks: thy heer es like a vlock of gooats what do appeer from Mount Gilyad.

Thy teeth es like a vlock of sheep that es aiven sheered, which come up from the washin'; ev'ry waun of which do beer twens, and narry waun es barren 'mong 'um.

Thy lips es like a thrid of scaarlet, and thy spaich es fitty: thy temples es like a piece of a pomegranate wethin thy locks.

Thy neck es like the tower of Daavid built for a armoury, 'pon which theere do hang a thousan' bucklers, oal shields of mighty men.

Thy two brists es like two young roes that es twens, which do feed 'mong th' lilies.

Ontil th' day do break, and th' shaddas do fly away, I'll git away to th' mount'in of myrrh, and to th' hill of frankincense.

Thee'rt feer oal awver, my love; theere es no spot in tha.

Come weth me from Libanon, my spouse, weth me from Libanon: luck from th' top of Amana, from th' top of Shainir and Hermon, from th' lions' dins, from th' mount'ins of th' leopards.

Thee'st ravished my heart, my sester, my spouse; thee'st ravished my heart weth waun of thy eyes, weth waun chain of thy neck.

How feer es thy love, my sester, my spouse! how much

betterer es thy love then wine! and th' smill of thy ooint-
ments then oal spices!

Thy lips, Aw my spouse, drap like th' honeycomb:
honey and melk es onder thy tongue; and th' smill of thy
gaarments es like th' smill of Libanon.

Your eärbs be a geärden o' pomegranates, wi' sweet
fruits, camphire, an' spiknard.

Spiknard wi' saffron, sweet ceäne, an' cinnamon, myrrh
an' aloes, wi' all the best spices.

A springhead in geärdens, a well o' spring water,
a-flowèn vrom Libanon.

Aweäke up, O north wind; an' come on, O south; and
blow on my geärden, that the smell mid flow out. Let my
true-love come into his geärden, an' eat his chaïce fruit.

Song of Songs v

I'm a-come to my geärden, my sister, my bride: I've a-
gather'd my myrrh wi' my spice; I've eaten my bread wi'
my honey; I've a-drunk o' my wine wi' my milk; eat, O my
friends; drink deep, my belov'd.

I do sleep, but my heart is aweäke: 'tis the vaïce o' my
true-love a-knockèn. Open to me, O my sister, my true-
love, my culver, my spotless: vor my head is a-vill'd wi' the
dew; an' my locks wi' the drops o' the night.

I've a-took off my frock; how can I don en ageän? I've
a-wash'd my two veet: how can I sweil em?

Then my love took his hand off the hole o' the door, an'
my heart did yearn vor en.

I rose up to open the door to my love, an' my han's dripp'd
wi' myrhh; an' my vingers wi' sweet-smellèn myrrh, on the
knobs o' the bolt.

I open'd the door to my love, but my love wer a-gone:

my very soul zunk when he spoke. I sought en, but noowhere could vind en; I called en, he gi'ed me noo answer.

The watchmen that went roun' the town lighted on me: they het me, an' bruised me; the guards o' the wall did strip off my mantle.

I do praÿ o' ye da'ters o' Zion, that if yo do meet wi' my true-love, you'll tell 'n I'm a-pinen wi' love.

O what can be your true-love, mwore than another, you feäirest o' women? What can be your true-love mwore than another, that you do so eärnestly warn us?

My true-love is feiär, an he's ruddy; the foremost among ten thousand.

His head is the finest o' goold; his locks be a-curl'd, an' so black as the reäven.

His eyes be as doves by the rivers o' waters: a-wash'd all in milk, an' fitly azet.

His cheäks lik' beds o' spices, lik' mounds o' flowers; his lips be lik' lilies a-drippèn o' sweet-smellèn myrrh.

His hands be goold rongs a-zet off wi' beryl: his belly's bright ivory a-laid awver wi' sapphires.

His lags be as pillars o' marble, a-zet upon bottoms o' goold; his feäce is lik' Lebanon, chaïce as the cedars.

His mouth is most sweet; oh! most lovely. This is my true-love; this is my friend, O d'aters o' Jerusalem.

Song of Songs VI

Where is thy true-love agone, O feäirest o' women?

Where is thy true-love a-turn'd, that we too mid look vor en wi' thee?

My love's a-gone down to his geärden, to the beds o' the spices; to veed in the geärdens, an' gather the lilies.

I be my true-love's, my true-love is mine; he's a-veedèn among the lilies.

You be handsome, my true-love, as Tirza, comely's Jerusalem, dreadful's an army wi' flags.

Turn off your eyes vrom me, they've awvercome me: your heäir's lik' a vlock o' the gwoäts a-showèn vrom Gilead.

Your teeth lik' a vlock o' white sheep, a-come up vrom the washèn; each wi' a twin, an' not oone o' em barren.

As the rind o' pomegranate, do show your cheäks in under your locks.

There be dreescore o' queens, an' o' concubines vour, an' maïdens beyond all oone's reck'nèn.

But oone is my culver, my pure oone; her mother's oone child, the darlèn ov her that ha' bore her. The maïdens did zee her an' bless her; the queens an' the concubines praïs'd her.

Who is this that's a-lookèn vwo'th bright as the day-break, feäir as the moon, clear as the zun, dreadvul's an army wi' flags?

I went down to the geärden o' nuts, to zee the green eärbs o' the valley: to zee if the vine wer in blooth, the pomegranate in bud.

Avore I wer ever aweäre, my soul had a-meäde me lik' the chariots ov Aminadab:

Return, come back, O Shulamite; come back, come back, that we mid behold thee. What can ye zee in the Shulamite? A band o' two armies.

Song of Songs VII

How comely your vootsteps wi' shoes, prince's da'ter! the jeints o' your thighs be lik' jewels, the work o' the han's o' the skillfullest workman.

Your neävel is lik' a roun' bowl not empty o' liquor; your belly a-roun' heap o' wheat a-bounded wi' lilies.

Your breästes two roes in a twin.

Your neck is an ivory tower, your eyes lik' the vishpools o' Heshbon, by the geäte o' Bath-rabbim: your nose lik' the tower o' Libanon, a-lookèn towards Damascus.

Your head is lik' Carmel, an' the heäir o' your head is lik' purple; a king is a-held in its curls.

How feäir an' how winnèn be you, O my true-love, vor jaÿs!

Your tallness is straïght as a palm-tree; your breästes lik' bunches o' greäpes.

An' I zaid, I'll goo up to the palm-tree, an' pull down his uppermost boughs: an' your breästes shall be lik' a bunch o' the vine, an' the smell o' your nose be lik' apples.

An' the roof o' your mouth lik' the chaïcest o' wine vor my love, a-meäkèn the lips o' vo'k sound asleep vor to speak.

I be my love's, an' his leänèn's towards me.

Come, my belov'd, let's goo out to the vields; let's bide in the villages.

Let's goo up betimes to the vineyards; let's zee if the vine is in blooth, an' if the neesh greäpe is a-showèn, an' if the pomegranate do bud; an' there I will gi'e you my loves.

The mandrake do gi'e out a smell; at our geätes be all kinds o' good things, new an' wold, that I've a-stor'd up all vor you, my belov'd.

Song of Songs VIII

O that you were as my brother, a-zuckèn my own mother's breast! When I vound ye without I mid kiss ye, nor then be a-thought o' so lightly.

I would leäd ye, an' bring ye hwome into my own mother's house, that would teach me; I would give ye to drink o' spiced wine, o' the juice my pomegranate do yield.

His left han' is under my head, an' his right a-cast roun' me.

I do warn ye, O da'ters o' Jerusalem, not to stir, not to weäke up my love till he'd like.

Who's a-comèn on up vrom the wilderness, a-leänèn upon her belov'd? I awoke ye under the apple-tree; 'twer ther that your mother oonce bore ye: there she that bore ye brought vwo'th.

O zet me's a seal on your heart, as a seal on your eärms: vor love is as mighty as death, an' jealousy hard as the greäve; the fleäme o't's a fleämén o' vire, the vire o' the Lord.

Many waters can never quench love, nor floods ever drown it. If a man would gi'e all o' the wealth ov' his house vor love, it would all goo vor nothèn.

We've a sister, but small, wi' noo tetties: what shall we do vor our sister, the day we do vind her bespoke?

If she's a wall, we'll build on her buildèns o' zilver; if she's a door, we'll deck her wi' panels o' cedar.

I be a wall, an' my breästes lik' towers; an' then I did seem in his eyes as oone that vound kindnes.

Solomon had a vineyard in Baal-hamon; he let out the vineyard to keepers; every man vor the fruit o't to bring in a thousand pieces o' zilver.

My vineyard that's mine is avore me: O Solomon, you'll teäke a thousand, an' the keepers of the fruit teäke two hundred.

You that do dwell in the geärdens, your friends do gi'e heed to your vaïce; let me heär it.

Meäke heäste, my belov'd, and be lik' a roe or young hart on the mountains o' spices.

APPENDIX

Some versions of Psalm CXXIII

I have collected here a few examples of similarity and dis-
similarity within the narrow compass of one of the shorter
psalms. Since Luther's version is so good, and visibly the
origin of some of the phrases adopted in English, I thought
it useful to include it. It may be of interest that when
Henry Bull in 1577 translated Luther's commentaries on
the Psalms of Degrees, he found the Geneva text the most
appropriate. The only advance on Coverdale in 1611 is the
word contempt, taken from the Douai version, where one
might suspect it was a transliteration of Latin, but this is
not the case. The same word *contempt* drives out Coverdale's
despitefulness also at *Esther* 1. 18. The Douai last verse does
reflect Jerome's version; all the other English versions
agree with the Hebrew and with Jerome's alternative
Latin *'iuxta Hebraeos'*.

Coverdale (Common Prayer)

Unto thee lift I up mine eyes: O thou that
dwellest in the heavens.

Behold, even as the eyes of servants look unto
the hand of their masters, and as the eyes of a

maiden unto the hand of her mistress: even so our
eyes wait upon the Lord our God, until he
have mercy upon us.

Have mercy upon us, O Lord, have mercy upon
us: for we are utterly despised.

Our soul is filled with the scornful reproof
of the wealthy: and with the despitefulness of
the proud.

1611 (variations from Coverdale)

... so our eyes wait upon the Lord our God,
until that he have mercy upon us.
... for we are exceedingly filled with contempt.
Our soul is exceedingly filled with scorning
of those that are at ease, and with the contempt
of the proud.

Douai

To thee have I lifted up mine eyes, which dwellest in the
heavens.

Behold as the eyes of servants are on the hands of their
master, As the eyes of the handmaid on the hands of her
mistress: so are our eyes to our Lord God until he have
mercy on us. Have mercy on us O Lord, have mercy on us:
Because we are much replenished with contempt.

Because our soul is much replenished: reproach to them
that abound, and contempt to the proud.

Geneva

I lift up mine eyes to thee, that dwellest in the heavens.

Behold as the eyes of servants look unto the hand of their
masters, and as the eyes of a maiden unto the hand of her
mistress: so our eyes wait upon the Lord our God until
he have mercy upon us.

Have mercy upon us, O Lord, have mercy upon us: for we
have suffered too much contempt.

Our soul is filled too full of the mocking of the wealthy, and
of the despitefulness of the proud.

John Carryl

To thee I have lifted up my eyes, who dwellest in heaven.

As the eyes of servants watch their Masters hands.

As the eyes of the handmaid are fixed upon the hand of
their Mistress, so are our eyes upon the Lord our God,
till he takes compassion of us.

Have mercy on us, O Lord! have mercy on us; for we are
in the lowest degree of contempt.

Our soul is full of confusion being reproached by the high,
and despised by the proud.

Luther

Ich hebe meine Augen auf zu dir,
    der du im Himmel wohnest.
Siehe, wie die Augen der Knechte
    auf die Hande ihrer Herren sehen,
wie die Augen der Magd
    auf die Hande ihrer Frau,

so sehen unsre Augen auf den Herrn, unsern Gott,
  bis er uns gnadig werde.
Sei uns gnadig, Herr, sei uns gnadig:
  denn allzusehr litten wir Verachtung.
Allzusehr litt unsere Seele den Spott der Stolzen
  und die Verachtung der Hoffartigen.

SOURCES

1 William Tyndale's New Testament (1534)
   Basic text: Cambridge University Press, 1938,
   edited by N. Hardy Wallis for the Royal Society of
   Literature.

2 Coverdale's Bible (1535)
   Text: Bodleian S. Seldon c. 9 Auctor. y. 1.

3 Matthew's Bible (1537), the work of Tyndale.
   Text: Bodleian Bib. Eng. 1537c, l.a.

4 John Fisher (about 1545)
   Text: Bodleian.

5 Cranmer's Great Bible (1541)
   Text: Bodleian Bib. Eng. 1541 cl. I have corrected
   a few slight and undoubted misprints.

6 Geneva Bible (1560)
   Text: University of Wisconsin Press facsimile
   reprint 1969.

7 The Bishops' Bible (1568)
   Text: Bodleian Bib. Eng. 1568 b. 1.

Sources

8 Douai Bible (1609)
   Text: Heythrop College, c. 1609.

9 Authorized Version (1611)
   Text: Edinburgh 1830 edition.

10 Hugh Broughton (d. 1611) ed. John Lightfoot, *The Works of the Great Albionean Divine Mr Hugh Broughton* (1662)
   Text: Bodleian Th. B. 18.13.

11 John Carryl, *The Psalmes of David*, translated from the Vulgate (1700)
   Text: once in author's possession, now Heythrop College, London.

12 Edward Harwood, *Liberal Translation of the New Testament* (1678)
   Text: Bodleian 8°B.S.; L 236.

13 Benjamin Franklin (1779), *Works* ed A. H. Smyth (1907) vol 7
   Text: Bodleian 2335 e 90.

14 William Barnes, *Zong o' Solomon*, Dorset dialect version (1859)
   Text: Bodleian 302(g) 183.